I0802194

IMAGES
of America

YUMA PROVING GROUND

On the Cover: The Army's Test Facility. In 1963, the US Army renamed the expanding Yuma Test Station the Yuma Proving Ground. As the mission of the Yuma Proving Ground continued to expand, the Army designated it a major range and test facility in 1974. During this time, it was conducting various tests on ranges that covered more than 1,200 square miles. One of the tests was of the long-range weapons systems, subsystems, and ordnance of an M60 Patton tank. Variants of the Patton were the main battle tanks during the Cold War. After being used in Operation Desert Storm in 1991, they were replaced by the M1A1 Abrams. The type being test-fired in this photograph, taken in 1973, is an M60A1E3, which had been upgraded with the 105mm gun. (Courtesy of the US Army.)

IMAGES
of America

YUMA PROVING GROUND

Lt. Col. Scott Laverty (Ret.)

ARCADIA
PUBLISHING

ISBN 978-1-4671-0450-0

Published by Arcadia Publishing
Charleston, South Carolina

Printed in the United States of America

Library of Congress Control Number: 2019945721

For all general information, please contact Arcadia Publishing:
Telephone 843-853-2070
Fax 843-853-0044
E-mail sales@arcadiapublishing.com
For customer service and orders:
Toll-Free 1-888-313-2665

Visit us on the Internet at www.arcadiapublishing.com

To those who have served in the harsh desert environment now known as Yuma Proving Ground.

Contents

Acknowledgments 6

Introduction 7

1. The Early Years 9
2. Fort Yuma 17
3. Yuma Quartermaster Depot 31
4. World War II and the Desert Training Center 35
5. Camp Laguna 43
6. Yuma Test Branch 65
7. Yuma Test Station 85
8. Yuma Proving Ground 103
9. Into the Future 121

Bibliography 126

About the Organization 127

Acknowledgments

Since the US Army Yuma Proving Ground Heritage Center was founded, thousands of hours have been spent preserving the history and culture of the Yuma Proving Ground. Without those who labored selflessly, this book would not have been possible. I wish to thank the curator of the Yuma Proving Ground Heritage Center, M.Sgt. William Heidner (Ret.), as well as retired Sgt. 1st Class Vince Lacey, for their knowledge of the topic and their selfless support in use of the research library and archives at the Yuma Proving Ground Heritage Center.

I must also thank the Arizona Historical Society and the Yuma County Library District's Heritage Library, where Laurie Boone graciously provided access and support for research. The collection of numerous articles, documents, and pictures helped fill the gaps prior to World War II.

I must also recognize all of those at Arcadia Publishing who kept me on track with guidance and encouragement to make this book possible—thank you, Lindsey Givens and Caroline Anderson.

I would be remiss if I did not give credit to my family, especially my partner in life, Lauri Laverty, whose experience and education as a teacher has been invaluable.

Finally, it is impossible to recognize everyone, but thank you to all those at the Colorado River State Historic Park—Quartermaster Depot Museum, the General Patton Memorial Museum, the Fort Yuma Quechan Tribal Museum, the Sanguinetti House Museum and Gardens, the Yuma Territorial Prison, and the many others who have preserved our history.

INTRODUCTION

The Yuma Proving Ground's history is not only fascinating, it enlightens the reader on its enormous impact on the world. One example is the Global Positioning System (GPS), which is not only used in military systems, but in nearly every computerized device today. It has changed the way we travel and live, and was a revolutionary piece of technology in part because of the Yuma Proving Ground.

Before the Yuma Proving Ground was founded or even before the Army's occupation of the area, the desert region along the Colorado River that divides Arizona and California was originally inhabited by Native Americans. They thrived along the Colorado River for centuries until the first Europeans set foot on what would be called Yuma.

Beginning in 1540, Spanish explorers from New Spain were the first Europeans to reach the area known as Indian Hill. The Spanish explorer Capt. Hernando de Alarcón led the first expedition up the Colorado River from the Sea of Cortez and is credited as the first European to arrive in what is now Yuma. He has also been credited with giving the Yuma Indians their name.

Around 1680, the Catholic Church expanded its influence into the area with Fr. Eusebio Kino conducting expeditions to convert the Native Americans and establish missions. But it was not until around 1770 when Juan Bautista de Anza arrived by order of the government of New Spain to find a land route to link northern California to Sonora that Yuma was literally on the map. During this time, the Quechan Indians had control over the river crossing on the Colorado River. Upon arrival, de Anza established a friendly relationship with the Quechan, which resulted in a Spanish settlement near the river crossing. He continued his expeditions to Mission San Gabriel, and by 1774, the Anza Trail and Yuma Crossing were on the maps, paving the way for future settlements. After Mexico won its independence from Spain in 1821, border conflicts between Mexico and the United States began erupting, resulting in the Mexican-American War (1846–1848), which brought the Army to the region. At the end of the war Mexico had lost a third of its territory, including land that would become Arizona. Western expansion was now in full swing.

In 1850, the Army began settling in the area with the construction of Camp Calhoun and later Fort Yuma. It is believed that Fort Yuma was built on the same hill, Indian Hill, that Capt. Hernando de Alarcón utilized in 1540 to survey the area overlooking the river crossing, making it a perfect military location. In 1865, the Army expanded and built the Yuma Quartermaster Depot near the river crossing below Fort Yuma. This provided a point for riverboats traveling up the Colorado River to deliver supplies. From there, supplies were transported by wagons to the various outposts along the frontier. The Army continued operations of the Yuma Quartermaster Depot and Fort Yuma until 1883. Today, the Quartermaster Depot is a museum that has preserved its history, and Fort Yuma now operates as the seat of the Quechan Tribe.

In 1939, Adolf Hitler directed the German invasion of Poland, and in 1941, the Japanese attacked Pearl Harbor, thrusting the United States into World War II. The Army returned to the desert to prepare soldiers and equipment for war. With Gen. George S. Patton Jr. leading the mission, the Army identified western Arizona and southeastern California as the key location for troop training and equipment testing in 1942. In a speech by General Patton to his troops in the same year, he stated:

> The war in Europe is over for us. England will probably fall this year. Our first chance to get at the enemy will be in North Africa. We cannot train troops to fight in the desert of North Africa by training in the swamps of Georgia. I sent a report to Washington requesting a desert training center in California. The California desert can kill quicker than the enemy. We will lose a lot of men from the heat, but training will save hundreds of lives when we get into combat. I want every officer and section to start planning on moving all our troops by rail to California.

In 1942, the Desert Training Center expanded into Arizona with Camp Laguna, a critical training site for preparing soldiers for combat. As the Desert Training Center was being established, the US Army Corps of Engineers identified a site just north of the Yuma River crossing and south of the Laguna Dam on the Colorado River as the best location to conduct bridge testing in 1943. The new site would be called the Yuma Test Branch, and would allow engineers to conduct testing of combat bridges and equipment in support of the war effort.

After World War II ended, the Yuma Test Branch transitioned from bridge testing to testing equipment in the desert environment in support of future military operations. The Yuma Test Branch continued to test equipment until 1949, when it was closed and then reopened as the Yuma Test Station in 1951. Maintaining its previous river and desert environment testing on military equipment, it expanded to artillery, armored vehicles, and air delivery systems testing.

In 1963, the Yuma Test Station was renamed the Yuma Proving Ground, and in 1974 was designated a major range and test facility by the Army. The Yuma Proving Ground's mission was expanded with the reassignment of aircraft armament testing from Aberdeen Proving Ground.

As the Army's premier artillery testing range with over 1,200 square miles, the Yuma Proving Ground has been hosted the Department of Defense and allied forces in testing equipment. One of these tests was the High Altitude Research Project (HARP), which fired a projectile to an altitude of 111 miles. In 1971, the Yuma Proving Ground expanded again with the creation of the most sophisticated helicopter armament testing range in the United States. Since then, it has continued to expand to test the military equipment that defends the nation.

Today, the Yuma Proving Ground's mission is to "plan, conduct, assess, analyze, report and support developmental tests, production tests, and integrated developmental and operational tests; and provide training support to Army, sister services, Department of Defense, US Government, international, and commercial customers."

One

The Early Years

The desert region along the Colorado River that divides Arizona and California was originally inhabited by Native Americans. In 1540, New Spain appointed Capt. Hernando de Alarcón to lead an expedition from the Sea of Cortez to the north. His mission was to provide supplies for Coronado's troops and locate the river that led to the sea. After several months, he located the mouth of the Colorado River. He launched his boats up the river, becoming the first European to reach the area known today as Yuma. Surveying the valley from a hill (Indian Hill) that overlooked the river, he saw the valley full of smoke from the open fire pits of the Native Americans and gave them the name "Yumas," from the Spanish word *humo*, meaning "smoke."

In 1662, Fr. Eusebio Francisco Kino led the California Expedition into the lands that were awarded to the Spanish crown by the Catholic Church. His mission, in part, was to convert the indigenous people and expand the church's influence by establishing missions. By the time of his death in 1711, he had established numerous missions and increased the agricultural skills of the native people. His explorations produced the standard reference map for the area, which assisted many later travelers through the desert region.

In 1770, Juan Bautista de Anza arrived by order of New Spain to find a land route to link northern California to Sonora. He established a friendly relationship with the Quechan Indians, who controlled the river crossing. By 1774, the Anza Trail and Yuma Crossing were on the map. After Mexico won its independence from Spain in 1821, explorers, missionaries, and settlers continued to cross at this location along the trail where the river allowed for safer crossings. After the Mexican-American War in 1848, settlement increased as the California Gold Rush began. An Army unit was assigned to the region to provide security to travelers and to quell regional conflicts.

In 1862, Colorado City was renamed Arizona City as riverboats began operating along the river to carry in supplies. The area flourished and continued to grow. In 1875, the Arizona Territorial Prison was established, further increasing the population. It was now a booming western town.

MONUMENT TO THE 1540 SPANISH EXPEDITION. Located on Quechan tribal grounds just west of Yuma and north of Mexico on Highway 186, this monument marks the historic expedition of the first Europeans into the area along the Colorado River. The monument reads in part, "Spaniards led by Hernando de Alarcon ascended the Colorado River by boat from the Gulf of California past this point, thereby becoming the first non-Indians to sight Alta California on September 5, 1540." Although Coronado did not discover the fabled Lost Cities of Gold, the expedition paved the way for future expeditions that would lead to settlements and military outposts in the region. The monument was placed in 1982. (Author's collection.)

Pilot Knob. Pilot Knob is the remains of the magma core of an ancient volcano that has since eroded away. Since the arrival of the Spanish explorers, this summit has been used as a landmark for river and land navigation, which is how it received its name. Located just west of the Colorado River in Imperial County, California, the summit's name has been commonplace in the area since World War II. Near the California Highway Patrol office in Felicity and north of the summit, General Patton established a camp as part of his Desert Training Center and named it Camp Pilot Knob after the summit. Since then, others have used the name, including the Pilot Knob RV Park just northwest of the summit. Today, the summit and parts of Camp Pilot Knob are controlled by the Bureau of Land Management, while other parts are controlled by the California Highway Patrol and private owners. (Author's collection.)

MONUMENT TO JUAN BAUTISTA DE ANZA. Juan Bautista de Anza led colonists in 1775 from New Spain to the area known today as San Francisco. His historic journey paved the way for future settlers, following what became known as the Anza Trail. The Anza Trail was designated a National Historic Trail by Congress in 1990. This statue of de Anza is a memorial to his contributions to the region. (Author's collection.)

NATIVE AMERICANS. The earliest settlers along the Colorado River were Paleo-Indians over 12,000 years ago. As the first Europeans arrived in the region, Native Americans were thriving: farming, fishing in local rivers and streams, and hunting the local wildlife. In this photograph, Arrow Maker and his daughter Kaivavit Paiutes are pictured in front of their home in northern Arizona. (Courtesy of the National Archives.)

YUMA INDIANS. With the arrival of Spanish explorers, the history of the region would dramatically change. In 1540, Captain Alarcón allegedly gave the Spanish name "Humos" to the local people because of the smoke he observed coming from their open fire pits along the Colorado River. This was pronounced "Yumas" by the natives. The Yumas consisted of local tribes in the region where the Quechan and Cocopah Indians reside today. (Courtesy of the Library of Congress.)

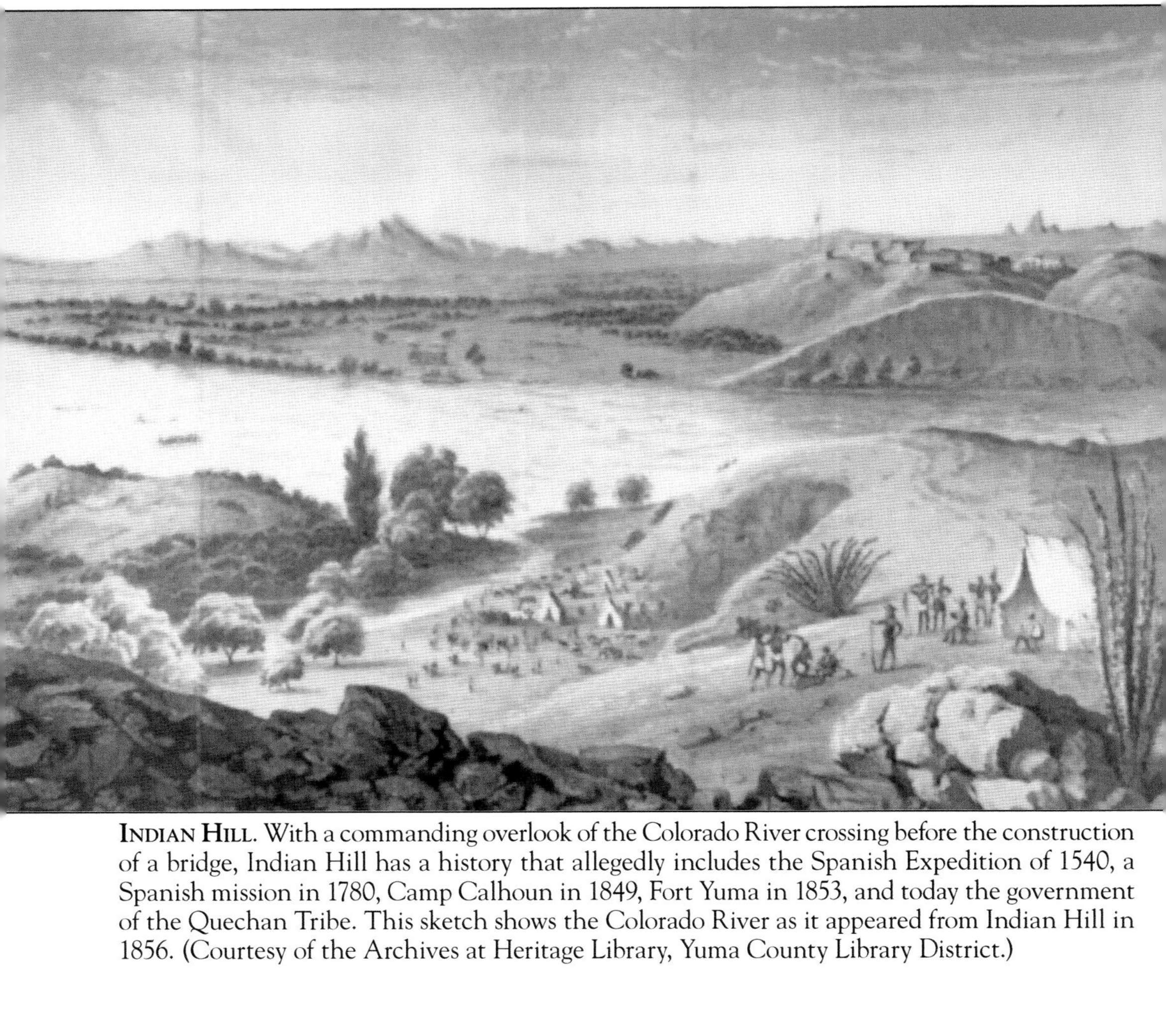

Indian Hill. With a commanding overlook of the Colorado River crossing before the construction of a bridge, Indian Hill has a history that allegedly includes the Spanish Expedition of 1540, a Spanish mission in 1780, Camp Calhoun in 1849, Fort Yuma in 1853, and today the government of the Quechan Tribe. This sketch shows the Colorado River as it appeared from Indian Hill in 1856. (Courtesy of the Archives at Heritage Library, Yuma County Library District.)

Settlements along the Colorado River. Since the late 1700s, explorers, missionaries, and settlers continued to move into the region. By 1870, the settlement along the Colorado River crossing was the largest in Arizona Territory. (Courtesy of the Archives at Heritage Library, Yuma County Library District.)

Regional Settlement Conflicts. With the arrival of settlers, tensions increased, and the Army was dispatched. In 1854, the inspector general of the Army, Col. Joseph Mansfield, stated in a report of Fort Yuma that "the Yuma Indians in this vicinity number about 300 warriors armed with bows and arrows . . . there are other Indians . . . within 150 miles—which, combined . . . might raise the number to 1,000 warriors." As settlers encroached on Native American lands, it was only a matter of time before conflicts erupted. (Courtesy of the Library of Congress.)

Army Outposts. The California Gold Rush of 1848 captured the imagination of people, and settlements were rapidly created across the frontier. To protect settlers, the Army established outposts along key routes. The Army also utilized outposts to travel across the frontier to conduct military operations. In this photograph, Maj. C.B. McLellan's camp is seen at Clear Creek, Arizona, while traveling to Fort Thomas, Arizona. Fort Thomas provided protection for the Gila Valley. (Courtesy of the Library of Congress.)

Two

Fort Yuma

On October 2, 1849, Camp Calhoun was constructed on Indian Hill as a campsite for the Corps of Topographical Engineers who were conducting boundary surveys. Named after John C. Calhoun, the 10th US secretary of defense, Camp Calhoun was under the command of 1st Lt. Cave Couts of the First Dragoons. The First Dragoons were responsible, in part, for overseeing the ferry services that provided river crossings to both military and settlers on the Colorado River.

On November 27, 1850, the US Army's 2nd Infantry, commanded by Capt. Samuel P. Heintzelman, was dispatched to protect settlers crossing the Colorado River. Camp Independence was constructed near the Colorado River crossing and operated until 1851. It was merged with Camp Calhoun on Indian Hill after a fire and renamed Camp Yuma. After establishing the camp, the 2nd Infantry departed on orders.

Camp Yuma was responsible for peace in the area, part of what was becoming known as the wild west. In December 1851, an uprising occurred requiring Major Heintzelman to return on February 29, 1852. Reoccupying the camp and putting down the uprising, he reestablished it as Fort Yuma. Peace was made with the local tribes by the end of 1852. Fort Yuma continued its mission until May 1883, when it was transferred to the Department of the Interior.

Monument to Fort Yuma. Located at Fort Yuma on Indian Hill where the Quechan Indian Tribe's museum is located, a monument stands to memorialize the history of Fort Yuma. It was placed on April 29, 1989. (Author's collection.)

The Yuma River Crossing. The location of the Yuma crossing was used as a trade route by the Paytans, a prehistoric people. With the Spanish arrival in 1540, the region became a point of future settlements. In the 1700s, battles over control developed, with the Quechans taking control in 1781. This photograph illustrates the width of the river and the conditions that made this a natural location for a river crossing. (Courtesy of the Archives at Heritage Library, Yuma County Library District.)

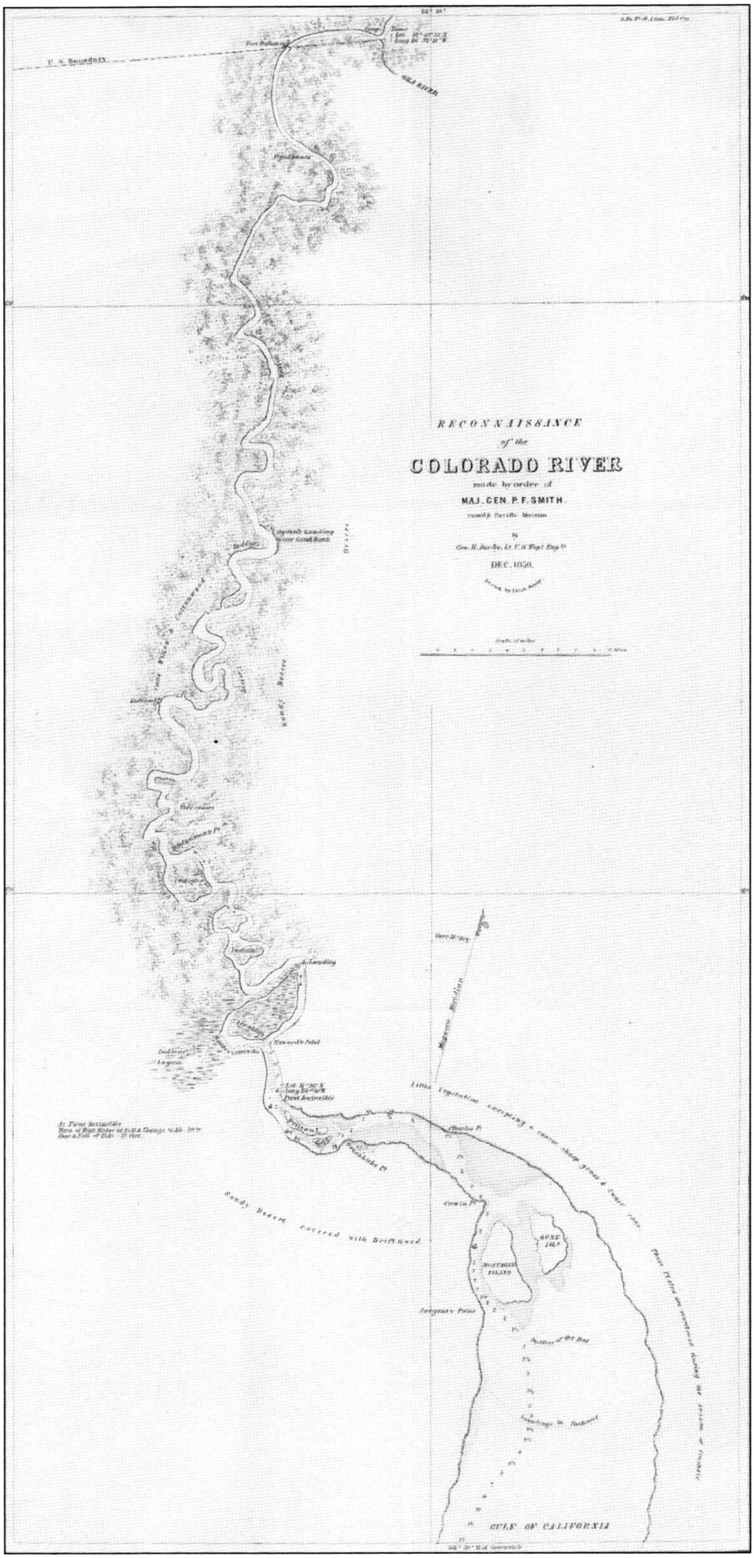

Reconnaissance Map of the Colorado River, 1850. As the Army established outposts across the frontier in the 1800s, the cost to supply them by land had become too high. In November 1850, Lt. George Derby, assigned to the US Army Topographical Corps, commanded an expedition up the Colorado River and created this map of the river, which was used for transportation. (Courtesy of the Colorado River Crossing Museum.)

Portrait of Gen. Samuel P. Heintzelman. General Heintzelman was a captain at the time he led the Army's 2nd Infantry in establishing Camp Yuma on November 27, 1850. After leaving, he did not return until 1852 when he was called back to reoccupy the camp. Upon retiring as a major general, he became the first president of the Sonora Exploring and Mining Company. (Courtesy of the National Archives.)

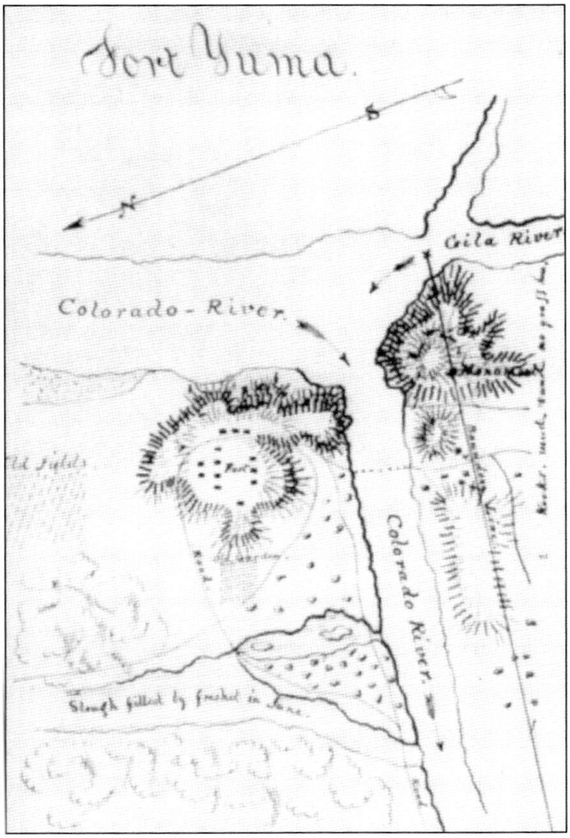

Terrain Sketch of Fort Yuma. The location of Fort Yuma on Indian Hill provided a commanding view of the area, which supported control of the Colorado River crossing and security for the fort. In 1854, Colonel Mansfield made this sketch of the terrain of Fort Yuma, revealing the importance of its location as a key military site. (Courtesy of the National Archives.)

Settlements of Fort Yuma. With the booming California Gold Rush and after the Mexican-American War, the US Army's role was expanded to protect both settlers and Native Americans across the frontier. The c. 1860 sketch above illustrates the early settlements on the Colorado River. The photograph below captures Mormon emigrants traveling by covered wagon in 1879. (Above, courtesy of the Archives at Heritage Library, Yuma County Library District; below, courtesy of the National Archives.)

The First Colorado River Crossing Ferry. Prior to a ferry on the Colorado River, crossing the river was slow and dangerous. In 1849, the California Gold Rush was in full swing and the first ferry to operate on the river arrived at the Yuma Crossing. Ferry owners in the region included Dr. A. Lincoln and L. Jaeger. Jaeger named a city on the west side of the river and developed a ferry that could carry a wagon across the river. Within the city of Jaeger, there was a hotel and store for travelers. Ferries continued to play a critical role in western expansion, taking travelers across the river until bridges and railroads were built. This photograph captures a group entering the ferry in preparation to cross the Colorado. (Courtesy of the Archives at Heritage Library, Yuma County Library District.)

Crossing the Barren Desert Terrain. By 1849, settlers were traveling across the barren landscape of Arizona Territory to reach the west. As it became common to travel with household goods, wagon transportation was the only reliable method. The Army also utilized wagons to resupply outposts across the region. The terrain in the region made transportation difficult by wagons. Eventually, the Army looked toward the Colorado River as a more economical method for resupply. The photograph above illustrates one of the dangers, and overturned wagon. Although taken later in 1903, the photograph below also captures the dangers of wagon travel, with a wagon seen in pieces at Canyon de Chelly in Arizona Territory. (Above, courtesy of the Archives at Heritage Library, Yuma County Library District; Below, courtesy of the National Archives.)

STEAMBOATS ON THE COLORADO RIVER. As the Army surveyed the Colorado River in the mid-1800s, steamboats began operating along the river, bringing supplies from the Gulf of California from 1852 to 1909 when the Laguna Dam was built. Here, a steamer anchors in front of Main Street in Yuma in 1898. (Courtesy of the Archives at Heritage Library, Yuma County Library District.)

YUMA RIVERFRONT STEAMERS AND SETTLEMENTS. Paddleboat steamers were an economical method to transport supplies between the Pacific Ocean and settlements along the Colorado River. Steamers would continue to operate as the most economical method until the building of the railroad in 1877. (Courtesy of the Archives at Heritage Library, Yuma County Library District.)

Camp Yuma Becomes Fort Yuma. In 1852, the Army's 2nd Infantry reoccupied Camp Yuma to provide protection to the camp and to the river crossing. In 1855, Camp Yuma was renamed Fort Yuma after a fire destroyed much of it. This etching illustrates the strength of Fort Yuma around 1860. In 1854, Colonel Mansfield inspected Fort Yuma. In his report, he stated that Fort Yuma was "one link in a chain of posts." (Courtesy of the Archives at Heritage Library, Yuma County Library District.)

Fort Yuma and the Civil War. In 1861, the Civil War broke out, and soldiers from Fort Yuma were dispatched to fight for the Union. The 1st California Volunteer Infantry was formed under Col. James Carleton with elements sent to Fort Yuma, maintaining control of the region. At the time of their occupation, Fort Yuma had a separate officers' quarters with a trail leading along the back of Indian Hill to give access, as shown in the later photograph above. In 1862, the 1st California Volunteer Infantry marched against the Confederate army between Fort Yuma and Texas, expelling the Confederates and taking control of the region. Col. James Carleton is pictured at right. (Above, courtesy of the Archives at Heritage Library, Yuma County Library District; right, courtesy of the Library of Congress.)

Fort Yuma and Arizona City. As settlements increased in the area, Jaeger City, which was located on the west side of the river, and Colorado City, on the east side, emerged. In 1862, a flood destroyed both cities. Colorado City rebuilt as it expanded, becoming Arizona City. The c. 1865 photograph above shows an early view of Arizona City. Below is a drawing of Fort Yuma's barracks. (Above, courtesy of the Heritage Center, Yuma County Library District; Below, courtesy of the Library of Congress.)

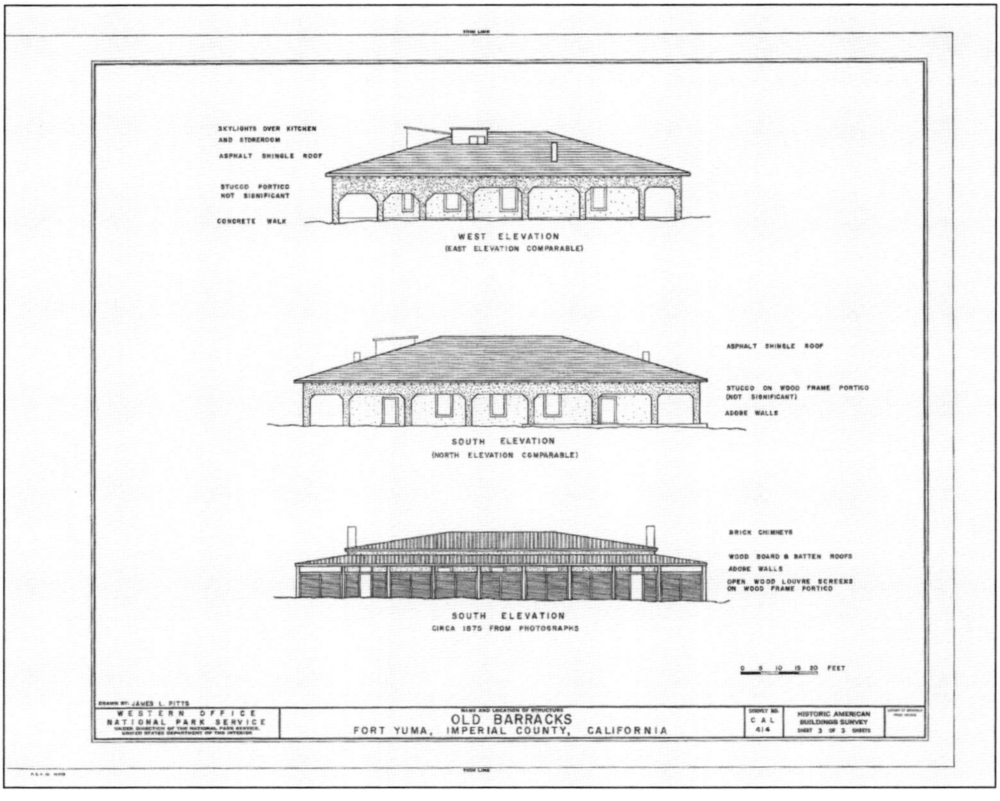

EXECUTIVE ORDER TO TRANSFER FORT YUMA. On January 9, 1884, an executive order was issued to assign Fort Yuma from the War Department to the Department of Interior, Office of Indian Affairs. This letter from the secretary to the commissioner of Indian affairs on February 2, 1884, directs that Fort Yuma be established as a reservation in the state of California for the Yuma Indians in lieu of a reservation by a previous executive order dated July 6, 1883, in the territory of Arizona. The photograph below shows Fort Yuma in the early 1900s, the location of the Quechan tribal government. (Right, courtesy of the National Archives; below, courtesy of the Archives at Heritage Library, Yuma County Library District.)

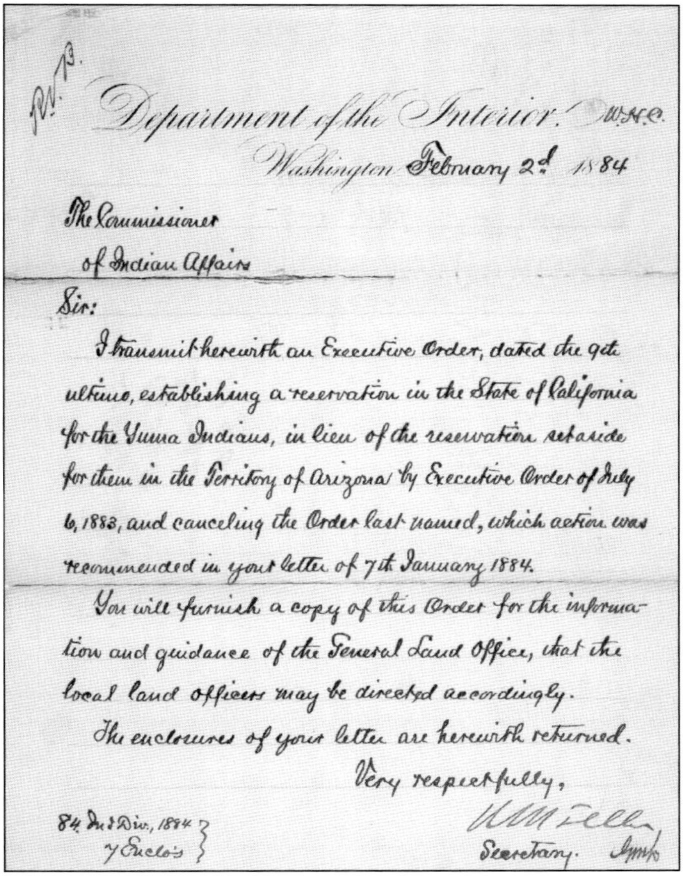

Department of the Interior. W.H.C.
Washington February 2d 1884

The Commissioner
of Indian Affairs

Sir:

I transmit herewith an Executive Order, dated the 9th ultimo, establishing a reservation in the State of California for the Yuma Indians, in lieu of the reservation set aside for them in the Territory of Arizona by Executive Order of July 6, 1883, and canceling the Order last named, which action was recommended in your letter of 7th January 1884.

You will furnish a copy of this Order for the information and guidance of the General Land Office, that the local land officers may be directed accordingly.

The enclosures of your letter are herewith returned.

Very respectfully,

Secretary.

84 Ind Div., 1884
7 Enclo's

Quechan's Fort Yuma. The frequent use of the Colorado River at Arizona City for crossing the river and receiving shipments of supplies meant sharing the area between the local Native Americans and the government. In the c. 1878 photograph above, a river ferry is seen on the far side of the Colorado with Fort Yuma in the background. A line ran across the river so the ferry would not be washed downstream. In 1884, Indian Hill was given back to the Quechan Tribe. Below is the Fort Yuma store with a Quechan tribal member sitting in front during the same year Fort Yuma was transferred to the Department of Interior, ending the Army's occupation at Fort Yuma in 1884. (Both, courtesy of the Archives at Heritage Library, Yuma County Library District.)

Three

Yuma Quartermaster Depot

In 1850, the Army completed its topographical survey of the Colorado River with confirmation from Lt. George H. Derby that the river could be navigated. In 1852, Capt. James Turnbull was awarded the first contract and became the first to provide riverboat transport for supplies. The commercial riverboating enterprise continued to grow on the river with several companies: George A. Johnson & Company (the *Colorado II* in 1862 and the *Cocopah II* in 1867), the Gulf of California Steamship Company (the *General Rosales* in 1878), the Colorado Steam Navigation Company (the *Cochan* in 1899) and the Mexican-Colorado Navigation Company (the *Retta* in 1900 and the *San Jorge* in 1901).

In 1854, Colonel Mansfield supported the idea of Yuma being a supply point for Army outposts when he stated in a report: "This mode of supplying will undoubtedly eventuate in making this post a sub depot for the supply of such post as will probably be established on the route to El Paso." Fort Yuma continued to receive supplies for the Army until 1865.

In 1865, the Army constructed the US Army Quartermaster Depot south of Fort Yuma along the Colorado River as the new supply point for the outposts along the western frontier. Military supplies continued to be shipped up the river to the depot and out to the Army outposts until the depot closed. With the establishment of the depot, Arizona City continued to grow in commercial trade. The Quartermaster Depot continued operations until 1883, when it was closed by the Army after the building of the railroad in 1877.

Today, the Quartermaster Depot stands as a museum, preserving local history and telling the story of the Colorado River.

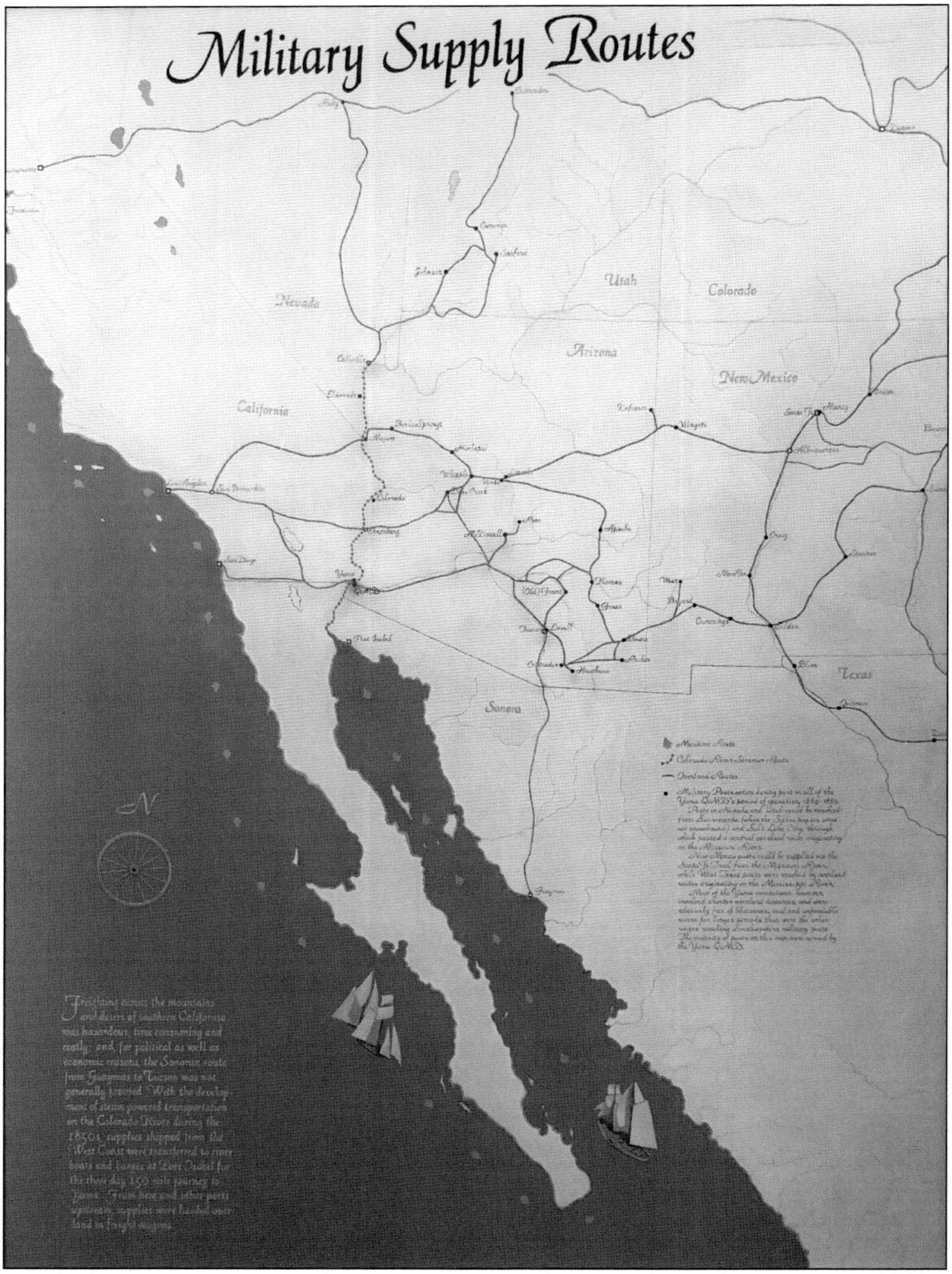

Military Supply Routes. After the Army's survey of the Colorado River led to the development of steamers operating on the river in 1852, the Army constructed the Quartermaster Depot at Yuma in 1865. The depot served as the lifeline to the Army's various forts and outposts across the western frontier, decreasing the costs of resupplying the Army from wagon transportation. The Quartermaster Depot could hold six months of supplies and continued to operate until the building of the railroad across the western frontier. Supplies were shipped up to the mouth of the Colorado River. From there, a steamer continued up the river to the depot. From the depot, supplies were transported overland to the various outposts and forts on the frontier. (Courtesy of the Colorado River State Historic Park.)

The Quartermaster Depot and Yuma. In 1854, the ratification of the Gadsden Purchase secured the Yuma area as territory of the United States. As the Civil War was ending in 1865 during construction of the Quartermaster Depot, increased commerce led to commercial development for Arizona City, leading to expansion. By 1873, Arizona City had recovered from the flood and renamed the settlement Yuma. This photograph captures the early city around 1880. (Courtesy of the Archives at Heritage Library, Yuma County Library District.)

Increase in Riverboat Transportation. As Yuma continued development with commercial enterprises, steamboats increased on the river. In 1850, the Army contracted with Capt. Alfred Wilcox to transport the schooner *Invincible* up the Colorado River. Although the schooner was unable to navigate up the river, it was determined that the river was navigable. In 1852, George A. Johnson partnered with Alfred Wilcox and Benjamin M. Hartshorne to form George A. Johnson & Company (later reorganized as the Colorado Steam Navigation Company in 1869). Their steamers would operate from the Sea of Cortez up the river 150 miles, delivering supplies to Yuma. As commercial industries grew, steamers continued to operate on the Colorado River until the building of dams. The photograph above captures the steamer *Colorado* (launched in 1862) near the foot of Main Street in Yuma. Below is the steamer *Cocopah II* (launched in 1867) at Norton's Landing. Both vessels were owned by George A. Johnson & Company. (Courtesy of the Archives at Heritage Library, Yuma County Library District.)

Four

World War II and the Desert Training Center

As the Nazis invaded Poland in 1939, the United States prepared its forces for the inevitable war that would come. On December 7, 1941, Japan attacked Pearl Harbor, forcing the United States into World War II.

With the attack on Pearl Harbor, the Army established airbases across the country to train pilots for combat missions. In 1941, the Army established the Yuma Army Air Base at Yuma's Fly Field, training pilots on the B-17 Flying Fortress and other aircraft. The Army also looked for a location to train soldiers in preparation for the ground fight with the Germans in the desert region of North Africa. Lt. Gen. Leslie J. McNair, the Army's chief of staff, assigned Gen. George Patton with the task. Since the United States had not engaged an enemy combatant in terrain like that of North Africa, Patton identified the Sonoran Desert as the training site.

Training began in 1942. The Desert Training Center continued to grow as military units reported for training. The first camp, Camp Young, was established by Patton in 1942 as his headquarters near Shafer's Summit, between the divide of Chuckwalla Valley and the Salton Sea. Camp Young was named after the Army's first chief of staff in 1840, Lt. Gen. Samuel B.M. Young. Other camps included Camp Coxcomb (1942–1944), Camp Rice (1942), Camp Granite (1943–1944), Camp Iron Mountain (1942–1943), Camp Clipper (1943), Camp Ibis (1943–1944), Camp Pilot Knob (1942–1943), Camp Hyder (1943), Camp Horn (1943–1944), Camp Bouse (1944), and Camp Laguna (1942–1944).

Today, the General George S. Patton Memorial Museum at Chirico Summit marks the historic location of Patton's headquarters, Camp Young, and displays relics along with telling the story of Patton's Desert Training Center.

The War against a Tyrant. According to the United States Holocaust Memorial Museum, over 42,500 Nazi ghettos and camps existed throughout Europe. More than six million people were killed. The world could not sit silently for long. America looked to put an end to Hitler's tyranny, and the training at the Desert Training Center supported that end. Between 1944 and 1945, the Allied forces liberated the camps. At left are inmates of the Amphing concentration camp in Germany liberated by US 3rd Army troops. Below is a portrait of Hitler in 1940. (Left, courtesy of the National Archives; below, courtesy of the Library of Congress.)

Attack on Pearl Harbor. On December 7, 1941, the Japanese attacked the US Navy's Pacific fleet at Pearl Harbor, Hawaii. Raids were conducted on Hawaii to prevent American fighters from getting into the air. As the Japanese attacked the runways, the ships at Pearl Harbor were hit. The USS *Arizona*, pictured here, was one of the many ships destroyed. (Courtesy of the Library of Congress.)

Declaration of War. The nation was shocked by the Japanese attack. The following day, December 8, 1941, Pres. Franklin D. Roosevelt declared war against Japan. (Courtesy of the Library of Congress.)

Join to Defend America. In 1941, the United States enacted the Selective Training and Service Act to provide for the defense of the United States by increasing the personnel of the armed forces. The act required men to register and be subject to military service. Those selected by a national lottery were drafted to serve on active duty for 12 months, followed by 10 years of reserve service. By the time the act expired in 1947, over 10 million men had been registered. Each military branch also conducted recruiting efforts to increase personnel for the war. Recruiting posters like this called for action. Many Americans were appalled by the attack on Pearl Harbor and volunteered to serve their country in the war against the Axis. Perhaps the most famous of the recruiting posters was this patriotic poster of Uncle Sam by James Montgomery. (Courtesy of the National Archives.)

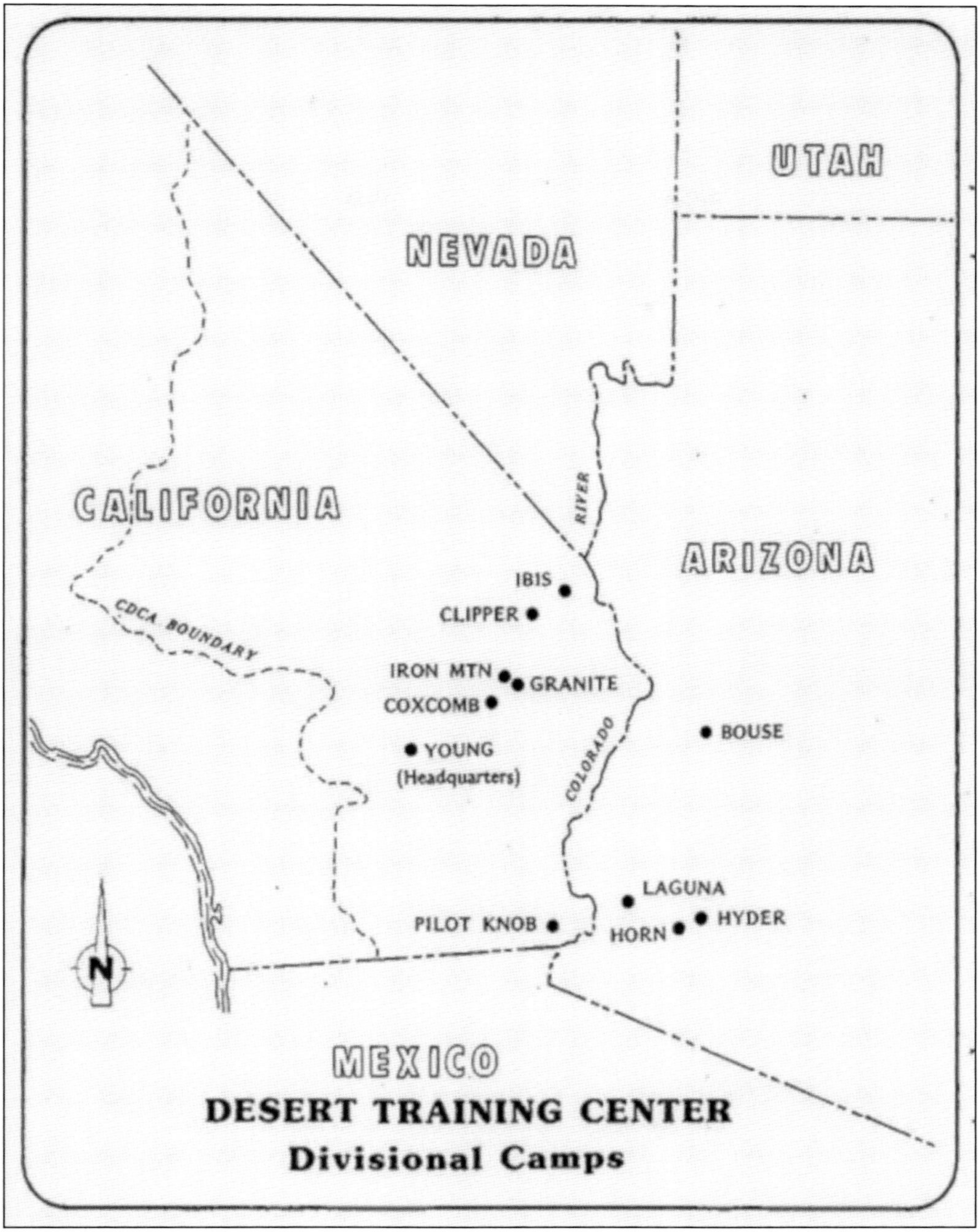

Map of the Desert Training Center. On February 5, 1942, Lt. Gen. Lesley J. McNair, Army chief of staff, approved the location of the Desert Training Center with General Patton as commanding officer. With his headquarters at Camp Young, Patton was the first commander of the Desert Training Center. The Desert Training Center expanded from eastern California to western Arizona and was approximately 100 by 200 miles in size. Most of the divisional camps were in California. Adding to the sometimes-violent sandstorms, temperatures in the desert could soar to over 120 degrees, testing both soldiers and equipment. The area was desolate, which reduced concerns that soldiers might attempt desertion. The training center began operations on April 30, 1942. (Courtesy of the Bureau of Land Management.)

The Desert Fox and the African Campaign. Gen. Erwin Rommel commanded the German 7th Panzer Division that won the battle with France. He was sent to the African theater to fight against the British, who were holding the Suez Canal. Taking the canal would mean naval superiority for Germany. Rommel earned the nickname "Desert Fox" with his famous goggles he had taken from British general Richard O'Connor after his capture in 1941. Rommel nearly pushed the British out before the Battle of El Alamein. The photograph above shows Rommel with the 15th Panzer Division in 1941. At left, General Patton addresses an audience before going on a training maneuver at the Desert Training Center in 1942. Patton served as commanding general until his departure on August 2, 1942, with Maj. Gen. Walton H. Walker assuming command. (Both, courtesy of the National Archives.)

Headquarters, Desert Training Center. The Desert Training Center consisted mainly of camps with temporary structures. However, General Patton's headquarters, Camp Young, had structures constructed of wood frames. After the war, most of them were torn down. The structures and encampment sites that exist today are protected. The above c. 1943 photograph shows Camp Young. Below is the entrance to Yuma Proving Ground where Camp Laguna once stood. Tank tracks, rock art, and tent outlines are common marks left on the desert from the Desert Training Center. (Above, courtesy of the General Patton Memorial Museum; below, author's collection.)

Monument to the Desert Training Center. Located at the General Patton Memorial Museum, this monument memorializes the history of the Desert Training Center. The monument reads in part, "The Camp, which began operation in 1942, covered 18,000 square miles. It was the largest military training ground ever to exist. Over one million men were trained at the eleven sub-camps (seven in California)." The monument was erected on November 11, 1989, by the state department of parks and recreation in cooperation with the General Patton Memorial Museum and the Bureau of Land Management. (Author's collection.)

Five

Camp Laguna

As Allied forces began to gain control of North Africa, the Desert Training Center transitioned in 1943 to a focus on combined arms and mechanized maneuver training in support of large-theater operations. Lt. Gen. Leslie McNair, commander of the Army ground forces, directed Maj. Gen. H. Walton Walker, commanding general of the California-Arizona Maneuver Area, to expand training for theater operations. The expansion brought training into Arizona and encompassed more than 18,000 square miles. The Desert Training Center had 12 camps that trained over a million soldiers for deployment into World War II.

Camp Laguna was the first to be built in Arizona and was considered the home to the 3rd and 9th Armored Divisions and the 8th, 79th, and 80th Infantry Divisions. Located approximately 28 miles north of Yuma, it was remote and barren, with extreme conditions. As units rotated through Camp Laguna, there were more than 10,000 troops being trained at any given time. Training assignments generally lasted for six months before being deployed to theater or reassigned. Camp Laguna was also home to the special bridge test section.

As the Yuma Test Branch was conducting bridge tests, more support was needed. After Italy surrendered to the United States, Italian prisoners who pledged their loyalty to the United States were sent to the Yuma Test Branch, where they formed two Italian Service Units and assisted in the testing of bridges from 1944 to 1945. Their contributions were significant, and a monument stands at the same location as the monument to the Yuma Test Branch.

Camp Laguna was not only significant in the history of training soldiers in preparation for deployment to combat, but also in the history of the Army's support to the Yuma economy. From the early settlements of Yuma, the Army's occupation to the area not only provided security, but also economical support, which has continued today. After Camp Laguna closed in 1944, the site was later absorbed by the Yuma Proving Ground.

RAILHEADS AND THE DESERT TRAINING CENTER. During the initial establishment of the Desert Training Center, the Sonora Desert had a number of railheads that could be utilized to transport personnel and equipment to the center. General Patton located camps close to railroads. Sites in California included Cadiz, Danby, Fenner, Freda, Glamis, and Goffs. Railroad sites in Arizona included Araby, Bouse, Dateland, Wickenburg, and Yuma. The Army's use of railroads created new challenges for the railroad companies, with a sudden increase in personnel and equipment transport. In the above 1943 photograph, the Freda railhead on California Highway 62 served as a railhead and campsite for the Desert Training Center. Below, tanks are being prepared at the Indio rail yard in 1942. (Both, courtesy of the General Patton Memorial Museum.)

The California-Arizona Maneuver Area. As the North African campaign ended, desert training was no longer required, and the Army began conducting combined arms and maneuver training. With the new focus, the Desert Training Center was re-designated the California-Arizona Maneuver Area in 1943. Combined arms and maneuver training is a military term that means combining different weapons systems to concentrate power on the enemy. This photograph shows an M551 Sheridan with "R&D Pilot No. 1" on the side. (Courtesy of the US Army.)

Leader Mentorship by General Patton. As the United States entered World War II, Lt. Gen. Walton Walker, nicknamed "Bulldog," took command of the 3rd Armored Division. In 1942, he took command of the 4th Armored Corps, which was re-designated the 10th Corps in 1943. In 1944, he led the 10th Corps (XX Corps) across France as part of General Patton's 3rd Army, distinguishing himself because of his tactics and speed, and receiving his third star. Before his deployment to the theater, he trained his unit at the Desert Training Center, receiving mentorship from Patton. He was a loyal soldier trusted by Patton. Here, Patton and Walker review a maneuver in 1942 at the Desert Training Center before deploying to the theater. (Courtesy of the General Patton Memorial Museum.)

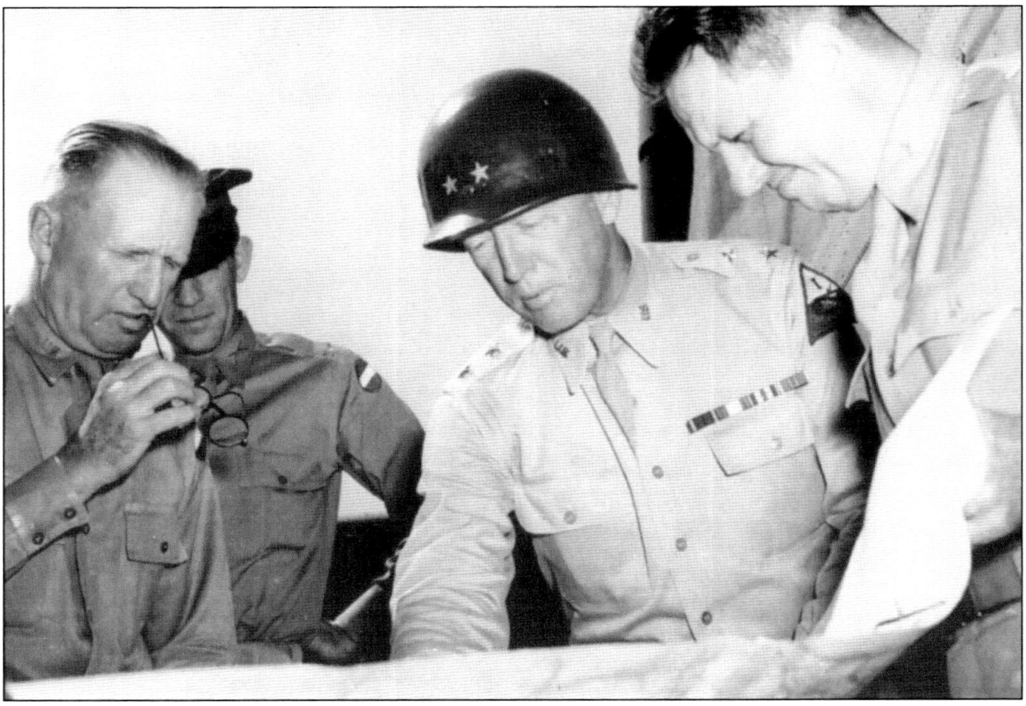

Conducting Realistic and Tough Training. According to the Yuma Proving Ground Heritage Center, "General Patton's prime responsibility with the first troops sent to the Desert Training Center was to test and increase their physical endurance." As troops trained, their leaders trained with them. Here, Generals McNair and Patton review plans in 1942 at the Desert Training Center. (Courtesy of the US Army.)

Strict Training. With the Army experiencing shortages in its officer ranks, Gen. George Marshall, Army chief of staff, proposed a school to rapidly train officers. By 1941, the Officer Candidate School was training new officers at Fort Benning, Georgia. General Marshall's guidance was simple: "get down to the essentials, make clear the real difficulties, and expunge the bunk, complications and pondering; concentrate on registering in men's minds certain vital considerations instead of a mass of less important details." Gen. Omar Bradley, commandant of the Infantry School, oversaw the Officer Candidate School and instituted a method of "efficient organization, strict discipline and rigorous training." As candidates became second lieutenants, they took this concept with them, and there was no exception at the Desert Training Center, as General Patton also integrated the method in preparation for combat. Discipline at the Desert Training Center included strict water and food rationing to condition soldiers for the rigors of desert warfare. (Courtesy of the General Patton Memorial Museum.)

Training at the Desert Training Center. Training at the Desert Training Center included individual and collective training. Individual training included such tasks as weapon qualifications and bayonet training. This training, when combined in squads and platoons, became collective training—the integration of individual training into squad, platoon, company, battalion, and division training exercises. Squad and platoon training also consisted of training on weapon platforms that required more than one person to operate, such as tanks and artillery. At left, a soldier exemplifies the individual task with a bayonet at Camp Laguna. Below, soldiers train on artillery near Needles, California, in September 1942. (Left, courtesy of the US Army; below, courtesy of the General Patton Memorial Museum.)

Training Maneuver Briefs and Formations. The Army conducts formations for various occasions, including troop movement and training, promotions and inspections, and leadership briefs. When flags were displayed, it represented a formal function of the command. It was also common to conduct after-action reports and briefs that captured both training and mission successes and failures. Above, soldiers listen to an after-action brief after conducting a maneuver exercise near Needles in September 1942. Below, soldiers stand in formation with flags displayed. (Courtesy of the General Patton Memorial Museum.)

ENTERTAINMENT AT THE DESERT TRAINING CENTER. The USO and other organizations brought entertainment to the camps. Soldiers would also write, play cards, and visit the nearby towns for. Although rigorous training was the model, recuperation was important for morale. In addition to Army training, camaraderie and lifetime friendships were established among many of the troops at the Desert Training Center. Above, this theater operated at the Desert Training Center to provide entertainment for the troops. Below, a group of soldiers joke while enjoying a break at a training site. (Both, courtesy of the General Patton Memorial Museum.)

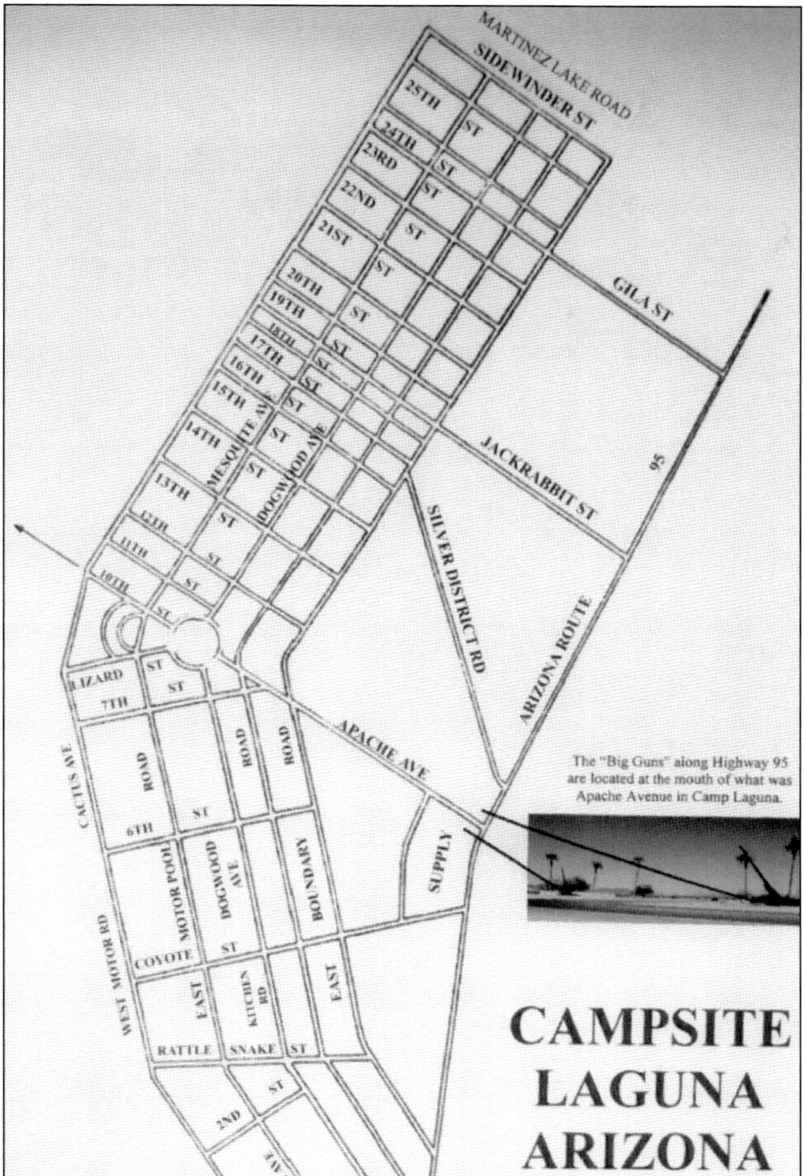

DESERT TRAINING CENTER, CAMP LAGUNA. As an integral part of a divisional camp during the Desert Training Center's expansion, Camp Laguna was established in 1942. This map shows the layout of Camp Laguna in 1943. With the new designation as the California-Arizona Maneuver Area, Camp Laguna saw its first division report for training in 1943, the 8th Infantry Division. This map shows Camp Laguna's campsite along Highway 95 in 1943. (Courtesy of the US Army.)

ENTRANCE TO CAMP LAGUNA. As units traveled from the railheads to Camp Laguna along Highway 95, they came to the main roadway, where they would enter Camp Laguna. Camp Laguna was set up by units, allowing for units to report and occupy their campsite. This photograph shows the tents aligned near Highway 95 at Camp Laguna around 1943. (Courtesy of the US Army.)

Military and Unit Pride. After occupying the campsite, the units often would mark it as their own with signs, rock displays, and other personalization. This was especially the case with General Patton's troops. Soldiers assigned to Patton's unit were disciplined and devoted. Patton instilled pride in the hearts of his soldiers with his personal belief that being a soldier was the highest profession and the greatest privilege in life. This c. 1943 photograph at Camp Laguna shows rock art made by soldiers in front of their campsite, displaying pride in their unit. (Courtesy of the US Army.)

LIVING CONDITIONS AT CAMP LAGUNA. The Army's campsites were standardized based upon the type of unit. The Army issued basic equipment to the unit and soldier for combat deployment in support of their mission. The photograph above taken at Camp Pilot Knob in 1943 captures what a soldier's basic living quarters looked like in the camps from 1942 to 1945. The photograph below shows a typical campsite layout in the desert at the Desert Training Center with rows of tents at Camp Laguna in 1943. (Courtesy of the Heritage Center Yuma County Library District.)

Camp Laguna's Campsites. As units transferred out, new units transferred in to the campsites established by the Desert Training Center/California-Arizona Maneuver Area. Camp areas in other parts of the United States had wood planks along the front of tent entrances to create a sidewalk. The tough conditions at the Desert Training Center did not support clean living conditions. Rather, the conditions prepared soldiers for the life they would experience in combat. In this photograph from 1943, tents at Camp Laguna are seen with the sides raised, a common practice to promote airflow because of the extreme heat. (Courtesy of the US Army.)

TRAINING THE MIND FOR COMBAT. General Patton focused on simplicity, so that a solider could remember and master skills to win the war. He focused on simple discipline of the essentials, which made him known for speed in combat. He always concerned himself with the welfare of the troops, which is why he required soldiers in his command to wear their helmets in the desert heat while training. To Patton, preparing for war included training the mind. That included wearing the proper uniform while at the Desert Training Center. In this c. 1943 photograph, a soldier stands at Camp Laguna wearing his Army uniform. (Courtesy of the US Army.)

The Army Uniform. In 1941, the Army issued the standard olive drab wool (winter) or khaki (summer) shirt with two large pockets, trousers that matched, canvas leggings, and a cotton field jacket. This soldier at Camp Pilot Knob in 1943 displays the standard uniform. (Courtesy of the Archives at Heritage Library, Yuma County Library District.)

Preparing for Training. After a unit arrived at a training camp at the Desert Training Center, they would unload their supplies and equipment and occupy the camp. It was common for soldiers to take smoke breaks during training, as seen here in 1943 at Camp Laguna. (Courtesy of the US Army.)

Camp Laguna Individual Training. Training at the Desert Training Center included individual training, such as individual weapon qualifications and training courses such as the Infiltration Course. Soldiers reporting with their units at Camp Laguna would have already received basic training in weapon marksmanship. Soldiers were issued the Colt .45 caliber M1911 pistol, as seen here in 1943 at Camp Laguna. (Courtesy of the US Army.)

EQUIPMENT TRAINING AT CAMP LAGUNA. Units at Camp Laguna trained with their equipment before deploying to the theater. Training was critical to prepare the soldiers for the rigors of war. Above, soldiers are conducting a reconnaissance patrol at the Desert Training Center. The Army used Willys MB and Ford GPW 4x4 jeeps from 1941 to 1945. Over 640,000 jeeps were produced during World War II. (Courtesy of the Library of Congress.)

Maneuver Training Campsites. As units conducted training across the Sonoran Desert, training exercises could last days. Soldiers would set up camps in the field while conducting operations, teaching critical survival skills. Above, a unit's jeeps are parked in front of the main camp. Below is the campsite of a unit conducting training at Camp Laguna around 1943. (Both, courtesy of the US Army.)

Camp Laguna's Exchanges. The Desert Training Center's camps were set up with tents that provided living space, headquarters space, supply space, and other support spaces. These photographs show soldiers enjoying a break at the exchange in Camp Laguna. A military exchange is a small store where soldiers can purchase basic goods. (Both, courtesy of the US Army.)

Standards of Physical Fitness. Early in training at the Desert Training Center, General Patton established high expectations for Army leadership. Officers would conduct daily physical training to condition their bodies with the constraints of rationed food and water in the desert climate. Training for war was critical to ensure the Army's success. Here, a unit first sergeant is seen eating with the troops. It is customary for Army leadership to live, eat, train, and fight together as a team with the troops. (Courtesy of the US Army.)

MONUMENT TO CAMP LAGUNA. Camp Laguna operated as one of the Desert Training Center campsites from April 1942 to April 1944. It left a legacy of testing equipment and training personnel in the harsh desert climate. This monument was erected in 1998. (Author's collection.)

Six

Yuma Test Branch

The war against the Axis brought a need for tactical bridging, and the Army looked for a location to conduct tests. In January 1943, the US Army Corps of Engineers identified a location along the Colorado River where the river flow could be controlled for equipment testing. The location was west of Camp Laguna and south of the Laguna Dam. The Yuma Test Branch's research on combat bridges contributed to the Allies' success against Germany during World War II.

A monument stands at the location of the bridge test site west of the Yuma Proving Ground and east of the Colorado River on East Imperial Dam Road erected by the Corps of Engineers. According to the monument, the following units supported the Yuma Training Branch: the 87th, 88th, 553rd, and 555th Engineer Battalions (Heavy Pontoon); the 527th Engineer Company (Light Pontoon); the 993rd Engineer Company (Steel Treadway); and Company E, 33rd Engineer Battalion (Armored). These units provided the support needed to conduct the tests, which improved bridging capabilities in World War II.

In 1944, the Yuma Test Branch expanded its studies to add hemp and rice plants for testing terrain maneuverability in preparation for an invasion of Japan. As the war came to an end in 1945, the Yuma Test Branch added mobility and equipment testing in the desert environment, becoming an active Army station. Facilities were constructed in 1947 as the Yuma Test Branch continued its research on combat bridging while also expanding until 1949.

With the expansion of the installation, the Yuma Test Branch was renamed the Yuma Test Station in 1951.

Monument to the Yuma Test Branch. Located just west of the Yuma Proving Ground, this monument memorializes the World War II bridge test site and reads, in part, "Transportation equipment for bridges was tested in the desert as well as in the dunes west of Yuma. The site continued to be used after the war, and permanent structures were erected in what is now the Headquarters area of the Yuma Proving Ground. The Test Branch was closed in 1949 and reopened in 1951 as the Yuma Proving Ground." (Author's collection.)

Test Facilities of the Yuma Test Branch in 1947. The Yuma Test Station was established in 1943 to test river bridging during World War II. In 1947, the Army expanded the role of the Yuma Test Station, adding mobility and desert environment testing. This is an aerial view of the Yuma Test Station in June 1947. The photograph is labeled as follows: (1) Floating Bridge Controlled Velocity Test Channel, (2) Bridge Impact Test Site, (3) Bridge Ultimate Capacity Test Site, (4) Bridge Trestle Test Site, (5) Bridge Test Pool, (6) Special Engineer Test Pool, (7) Marine Power Section, (8) Soils Trafficability Test Site, (9) Troop Area, (10) Motor Pool, and (11) New Campsite Access Road. (Courtesy of the US Army.)

T-92 240MM HOWITZER TESTING. As the United States prepared to invade Japan, the T-92 was designed as a weapon that could destroy Japanese bunkers built into the ground. Nicknamed "King Kong," it weighed more than 65 tons and was sent to the Yuma Test Station to determine if combat bridges could support the armored vehicle. The photograph above shows a T-92 being loaded onto a seven-pontoon reinforced M4 raft that was propelled by a 25-foot utility powerboat. The photograph below shows an 80-ton trestle being tested for maximum stress with the T-92. Research of trestles to test their abilities included both floating and fixed bridges. (Both, courtesy of the US Army.)

Test Facilities of the Yuma Test Branch, 1948. On July 26, 1948, the Army took this aerial photograph of the construction at the Yuma Test Branch. The numbers indicate the location of sites as follows: (1) Colorado River; (2) Soils Trafficability Site; (3) Fixed Bridge Ultimate Capacity Site; (4) Bridge Sub-Section, Field Office and Shops; (5) Bridge Impact Test Site; (6) Post Engineer Facilities; (7) Swampy Terrain Bridge Test Site; (8) Floating Bridge, Ultimate Capacity Site; (9) Bridge Trestle Test Site; (10) Special Engineering Field Office and Yard; (11) Motor Pool; (12) Service Bridge; (13) Floating Bridge Controlled Velocity Test Channel; (14) Present Troop Area; (15) Post Engineer Facilities; (16) Imperial Dam; (17) Fire Station; (18) Gila Canal; (19) Marine Power Facilities; and (20) All American Canal. (Courtesy of the US Army.)

Inspection of the Yuma Test Branch. As World War II came to an end, the Army expanded the mission of the Yuma Test Station in 1947. In November 1948, an inspection of the new construction took place at the Yuma Test Branch by Maj. Gen. Douglas Weart, commanding general of Fort Belvoir and the Engineer Center. The result was a report by Lt. Col. James Rorabaugh, commander of the Corps of Engineers. The information from the report is a significant part of the history recorded in this book on the Yuma Test Branch. The photograph to the left is of the inspection team. Below is an aerial view of the campsite on the Yuma Test Branch in 1948. (Both, courtesy of the US Army.)

Expansion of the Yuma Test Branch. This is an illustration of the construction plan for the new camp. The photograph is labeled as follows: (1) Chocolate Mountains, (2) Sand Dune Test Area, (3) Picacho Peak, (4) Old Senator Mine, (5) Trigo Mountains, (6) Village, (7) All American Canal, (8) Desilting Works, (9) Imperial Dam, (10) Reservoir, (11) Troop Area, (12) Ultimate Capacity Test Site, (13) Headquarters, (14) Diversion Channel, (15) Marine Power Section, (16) Bridge Test Pool, (17) Service Bridge, (18) Velocity Test Channel, (19) Special Engineer Test Pool, (20) Bridge Impact Test Site, (21) Soils Trafficability Site, (22) Colorado River, (23) Main Transmission Line, (24) Sewage Disposal, (25) Water Pump Station, (26) Motor Pool, (27) Gila Canal, (28) Warehouses, (29) Exhibit Building, (30) Mess Hall, (31) Cold Storage, (32) Headquarters, (33) Fire Station, (34) Power Sub-Station, (35) Flood Diversion Levee, (36) Post Engineer, (37) Admin Building, (38) Barracks, (39) Flood Control Channel, (40) Enlisted Club, (41) Housing, (42) PX/PO, (43) Pool, (44) Tennis Courts, (45) Housing, (46) Bowling Alley, (47) Infirmary, (48) School, (49) NCO Club, (50) Theater, (51) Storage Tank, (52) Chapel, (53) Housing, (54) BOQ, (55) Ball Park, (56) Housing, (57) Dormitory, (58) Housing, (59) Officers' Club, (60) Housing, and (61) Housing. (Courtesy of the US Army.)

YUMA TEST STATION, 1948. A bulldozer pulls a cable trailer over the Yuma Test Station terrain to the Research and Development Area during construction. Here, Sgt. Richard C. Delaney tends the cable reel on April 21, 1953. The speed of the wheel had to be consistent to prevent damaging the cable as it was rolled out, which would increase the cost of construction. Taken in 1948, the photograph below was taken as part of General Weart's inspection of the construction on the new camp. (Courtesy of the US Army.)

Task Force Furnace and the Laguna Army Air Field. The Army Ground Forces and Development Board developed a task force to research the effects of the desert environment on ordnance. Task Force Furnace arrived at the Yuma Test Branch in 1947 and began conducting tests in the desert environment to show how conditions would affect equipment. Pictured above is Task Force Furnace at the Laguna Army Air Field (LAFF). Below is the LAFF in 1954. The LAFF was built as an auxiliary airfield to the Yuma Army Air Field around 1943. (Both, courtesy of the US Army.)

Headquarters, Yuma Test Branch. Pictured is construction of the headquarters in 1948 for the Yuma Test Branch. (Courtesy of the US Army.)

Field Exchange, Yuma Test Branch. As the new camp for the Yuma Test Branch was under construction, a store was constructed called the Field Exchange. This store provided basic needs for employees as the Yuma Test Branch was being built in 1948. (Courtesy of the US Army.)

Bailey Bridge. The Bailey Bridge was constructed at the Yuma Test Branch to conduct both floating and fixed extensive tests. Shown here is a single/double traffic test crossing a waterway. (Courtesy of the US Army.)

Trafficking Impact Tests. This illustration of a complex bridge testing system was part of a study to determine the effects of traffic on military bridges. The system utilized an oscillograph to record 12 points that captured the sensitive impact factors of traffic. (Courtesy of the US Army.)

Bridge Impact Tests. At the Yuma Test Branch, the new camp continued research and tests on military bridges. Here, an impact study of a military bridge is conducted. (Courtesy of the US Army.)

Bridge Capacity Testing. On the structure shown here, a center connection is being tested to determine the maximum capacity of the bridge, along with its components. Using jacks and load meters, tank loads on the Bailey Bridge were transferred in definite increments to determine stress by visual evidence of failure indicated by test gages. (Courtesy of the US Army.)

VEHICLE LAUNCHED BRIDGES. The Yuma Test Station conducted research on tactical bridges that could be deployed by vehicle systems to rapidly bridge narrow gaps. Above, an M1 Scissor Bridge is being tested using a semi-trailer and hydraulic system. Below, a pontoon bridge is being constructed across the Colorado River during river crossing training. (Above, courtesy of the US Army; below, courtesy of the General Patton Memorial Museum.)

GOODYEAR RUBBER BRIDGES. Goodyear advertised the use of its products to support the war effort. The fact that America's enemies could destroy bridges, but it would do little to stop American forces from crossing was a product of the testing of the Yuma Test Branch. The Yuma Test Branch's research with America's industries supported victory in World War II. (Courtesy of the US Army.)

Bridge Capacity Tests. As research was conducted on bridges at the Yuma Test Branch, bridge load capacities in varying conditions were studied. Here, an M2 Steel Treadway Bridge is tested to determine safe load capacities with a moving M4 tank traveling at 8 mph in low stream current. (Courtesy of the US Army.)

Floating Bridge Tests. The M4 floating bridge was developed and tested at the Yuma Test Branch. In this picture, a T28 heavy tank with a weight of 124 tons crosses an M4 floating bridge. (Courtesy of the US Army.)

Water Debris Tests. The effects of river debris against floating bridges were tested at the Yuma Test Branch. Here, an M4 floating bridge is tested against the impact of debris from a current of eight feet per second. (Courtesy of the US Army.)

Pontoon Bridges. Research was conducted on floating bridges at the branch. Illustrated in this image is a tripartite pontoon bridge that was constructed from an M4 bridge being tested for the development of increasing the capacity and/or creation of a double lane roadway for normal capacity. The bridge shows a 150-ton load to simulate increasing capacity. (Courtesy of the US Army.)

Pneumatic Floats. The Yuma Test Branch conducted tests to determine military uses of pneumatic floats. The photograph above shows the testing of traffic wear between cotton and nylon in swampy terrain. Research on rafts was extensive at the Yuma Test Branch. Below, an M4A2 class 35 raft with a 20-ton load is testing the flow of the 18-ton pneumatic floats while being towed at 8.6 feet per second. (Both, courtesy of the US Army.)

M4A2 Floating Bridge. With research comes trial and risk. During an M4A2 floating bridge (raft) high-velocity test at 10.5 feet per second on January 28, 1948, the M4A2 failed and was washed down the river. The photograph above shows it being tested. Below, the M4A2 collides with a tripartite pontoon bridge. (Both, courtesy of the US Army.)

Reconnaissance Boat. The Yuma Test Branch conducted an array of tests on equipment. In this test, a hooded M1 motorized pneumatic boat that could carry four personnel is being tested for reconnaissance operations. Designed to carry reconnaissance parties onto enemy shores, the boat could be launched from submarines or aircraft. (Courtesy of the US Army.)

Cable Testing. The development of propelling cables was researched at the Yuma Test Branch using various methods including rockets, mortars, launchers, anchors, and dispensers. This is a Navy rocket set to propel 1,000 feet of quarter-inch wire. (Courtesy of the US Army.)

Vehicle Testing. The Yuma Test Branch conducted vehicle testing in varied conditions. Here, a 20-ton semi-trailer that is front-loading with a power unit, towed by a six-ton prime mover is tested. The trailer's ability to power the trailer's wheels enhanced its ability to maneuver through difficult terrain. (Courtesy of the US Army.)

Terrain Testing. At the Yuma Test Branch, research of traffic maneuverability led to the discovery of improved mobility by deflating tires. Low-pressure tires in soft and rugged terrain in comparison to high-pressure tires was studied, which led to the improvement of off-road performance. (Courtesy of the US Army.)

Seven

Yuma Test Station

At the end of World War II in 1945, the Army began closing training camps and facilities. Because the Yuma Test Branch's capabilities contributed to the war effort, the Army kept the Yuma Test Branch open to continue testing. By 1947, the Army had begun to expand the Yuma Test Branch's mission by adding mobility and desert environment testing. In 1948, the Army began new construction at the Yuma Test Branch. In 1949, the Yuma Test Branch was closed, and in 1951, it reopened with the new name of Yuma Test Station. With the Yuma Test Station now a permanent facility, it was assigned to the 6th US Army.

From 1951 to 1963, the Yuma Test Station continued to expand its role in testing military equipment. This included air delivery systems, armored vehicles, artillery, drones, ordnance, and chemical testing. Under the new mission, the Yuma Test Station had the largest artillery range in the United States, conducting numerous tests.

The Yuma Test Station continued to expand its roles until 1963, when the Army re-designated it as one of only two Army proving grounds. With the re-designation came renaming, and Yuma Test Station became Yuma Proving Ground.

JAPAN SURRENDERS. On August 14, 1945, Pres. Harry Truman announced Japan's surrender to the United States. With World War II over, the Yuma Test Branch's success in testing and development during the war resulted in the Army expanding it. Closing in 1949, the Yuma Test Branch reopened in 1951 as the Yuma Test Station. This c. 1945 photograph shows Truman at his desk. (Courtesy of the Library of Congress.)

Aerial View of New Construction. In 1948, construction of the Yuma Test Branch was under way, as seen in the aerial photograph above. Permanent buildings including housing and entertainment facilities were being built as the Yuma Test Branch became a permanent station for testing military equipment and personnel. By 1951, Yuma Test Branch was Yuma Test Station. As the Army expanded the capabilities of the newly designated test station, the automotive test facility established courses to conduct tests throughout the year as equipment improved. Below is the automotive division on April 1, 1958. (Both, courtesy of the US Army.)

Boat Transportation. In addition to watercraft research at the Yuma Test Station, the ability to transport was studied to develop and improve methods. This 25-foot-long utility power boat is being carried over rocky terrain using a pintle hitch trailer with a launching device that was developed at the Yuma Test Station. (Courtesy of the US Army.)

Time Bruise Course. In the middle of the mountains, the Yuma Test Station's "Time Bruise Course" tested vehicles in the automotive division. In the 1950s, the Army was utilizing the M35 series cargo trucks nicknamed "Deuce and a Half." Here, a Deuce and a Half performs a tire test through the Time Bruise Course. (Courtesy of the US Army.)

Tank Gravel Course. An M26A2 truck-tractor pulling an M15A2 semitrailer loaded with an M48 tank is being tested on the tank gravel course in 1957, testing the payload capacity of the trailer. The Army's role of fighting the country's wars around the world requires the ability to deliver weapons systems in all types of terrain and can only be determined with testing. (Courtesy of the US Army.)

Sand Course. An XM408 three-quarter-ton 6x6 cargo truck is being tested in hummocky sand in 1959. Hummocky sand is a type of sedimentary material found in sandstone and often formed by large storms. The tests were conducted where the surface was irregular to test the equipment's capabilities for combat deployment in different types of terrain. (Courtesy of the US Army.)

Tank Hilly Cross-Country Course. To test the capabilities of combat vehicles to traverse different terrain and slopes, the Yuma Test Station developed a course that tested equipment from moderate to extreme terrain. Above, an XM408 three-quarter-ton 6x6 cargo truck is negotiating the tank hilly cross-country course in 1959. Below, a LVTP-X2 landing vehicle is being tested on the course in 1955. (Both, courtesy of the US Army.)

The Sand Slopes Course. As the Army conducted rigorous training for World War II at the various campsites at the Desert Training Center in 1942, the sand dunes that extend from the Sea of Cortez to the Salton Sea were identified as a desert test site, with Camp Seeley being established there. Located west of the Yuma Test Station, the California sand dunes were used to conduct extensive mobility tests on sandy terrain. Equipment was tested at varied slope grades to determine mobility. Tire pressures were studied as a means for improved mobility with each slope. Above, an M38 quarter-ton truck pulling an M416 trailer is being tested at the California Sand Dunes in 1951. Below, an M54 five-ton truck is being tested after the sand slopes test site was built in 1953. (Both, courtesy of the US Army.)

Project Otter. During the 1950s, overland trains were being developed with the capability to cross over various terrain, creating a direct logistical line anywhere, any time. The US Army conducted research on overland trains and in 1958 contracted for the TC-497 Overland Train Mark II. Completed in 1962, the TC-497 was transported to the Yuma Test Station for testing under Project OTTER (Overland Train Terrain Evaluation Research). Although the vehicle performed well across various terrain, it moved at a slow speed. The Army rejected the overland train over aviation lift capabilities as a supply delivery system and the TC-497 was sold off except for the control cab, which is displayed at the Yuma Proving Ground Heritage Center. The TC-497 holds the record for the longest off-road vehicle in the world. (Courtesy of the US Army.)

Mud Course. As the focus changed during World War II from North Africa to the European theater, the Army was required to fight through muddy and flooded areas. To test the ability of a combat vehicle to operate across waterways and wetlands, the Yuma Test Station developed the mud course. In the photograph above, an M60 tank is being tested at the mud course for its ability to traverse rivers. Below, an M59 armored infantry vehicle undergoes testing, which determined that it could not be controlled in deep mud, requiring alterations in 1955. (Both, courtesy of the US Army.)

Soils Trafficability Research. At the Waterways Experiment Station at the Yuma Test Station, soil classifications for trafficability were created. Soil classifications were critical for the Army's ability to conduct route reconnaissance by recon forces who operated ahead of the main forces to determine navigable routes. Route recon was often a task of the military police or infantry scouts once in the theater. The soil classifications were utilized for military planning. Here, sandy soil is being tested during the winter months. (Courtesy of the US Army.)

Testing Equipment for the Department of Defense. The Yuma Test Station conducted tests not only for the Army, but also for the Department of Defense. Equipment being considered for other military branches was at times sent to the Yuma Test Station as well. The station also tested equipment for allied countries. In 1955, the Yuma Test Station tested the LVTPZX2 landing vehicle for the US Marine Corps at the swimming test site. (Courtesy of the US Army.)

Slope Course. The Yuma Test Station developed another site to test the performance of vehicles on various inclines. Here, an Elke tank is tested on the slope course at a 60-degree incline to determine its capabilities. The Elke tank was an experimental project testing an oscillating gun on an M551 Sheridan hull. (Courtesy of the US Army.)

Tank Course. Armored vehicles were tested in various types of terrain utilizing existing sites at the Yuma Test Station as well as the local terrain. This T48E2 90mm gun tank is going through a performance test of its AUSI 1790 fuel injection engine in 1955. (Courtesy of the US Army.)

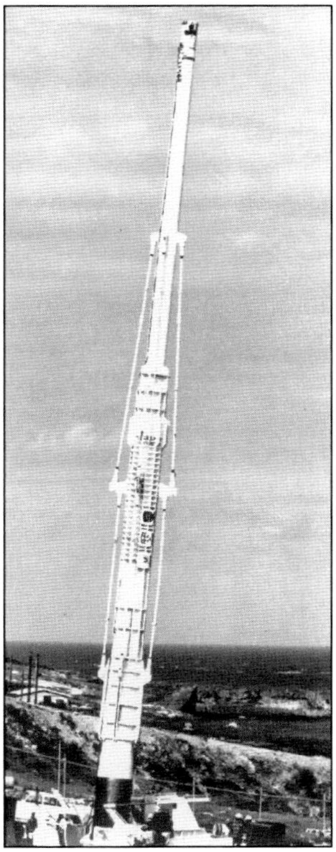

The High Altitude Research Project (HARP). Prior to the High Altitude Research Project, Canadian scientist Dr. Gerald Bull envisioned launching satellites into low earth orbit by firing them from a tube. A prototype was created from two 16-inch gun tubes taken off a Navy battleship and welded together. The Army's Ballistic Research Lab partnered with Dr. Bull as the Army was conducting research in the ionosphere. In 1963, the project was brought to the Yuma Test Station, where the second HARP gun was successfully tested. The photograph above is of a 16-inch naval gun firing at the Yuma Test Station. At left is the HARP gun that fired at near vertical with special projectiles being launched to approximately 110 miles high. (Both, courtesy of the US Army.)

AVIATION TESTING. In the 1950s, Fort Huachuca conducted drone tests for surveillance. In 1959, the Surveillance Drone Test Detachment was designated at the Yuma Test Station. The Yuma Test Station developed multiple airstrips for unmanned aerial systems. In addition to conducting bridge testing, mobility testing, and desert environment testing, the Yuma Test Station conducted aviation tests, which included armament testing, prototype aircraft testing, lift capabilities, and other tests. In the photograph above, a helicopter is conducting an armament test. Below, a drone test is being conducted in 1960. (Both, courtesy of the US Army.)

Surveillance Drone Testing. Before transferring the Surveillance Drone Test Detachment to the Yuma Test Station, Fort Huachuca flew drones over the Yuma Test Station to test them for battlefield operations. In the c. 1950 photograph above, the first drone for battlefield surveillance with the capability of taking pictures by radar is being tested. At left, an MQM58A drone is recovered from flight testing on March 13, 1964. (Both, courtesy of the US Army.)

Military Free Fall. "Military free fall" is the term used for the training that requires a jumper to manually deploy a parachute, unlike static jumps where the parachute is deployed upon leaving the aircraft by a control line. Military free fall consists of two basic techniques: The high-altitude low-opening technique (parachutist jumps at 10,000 feet, deploying the parachute at 4,000 feet) and the high-altitude high-opening technique (parachutist jumps at 30,000 feet, deploying the parachute upon stabilization). Both techniques give the operator the ability to descend onto enemy targets undetected. The Yuma Test Station conducted tests on parachute systems in support of military free fall operations. (Both, courtesy of the US Army.)

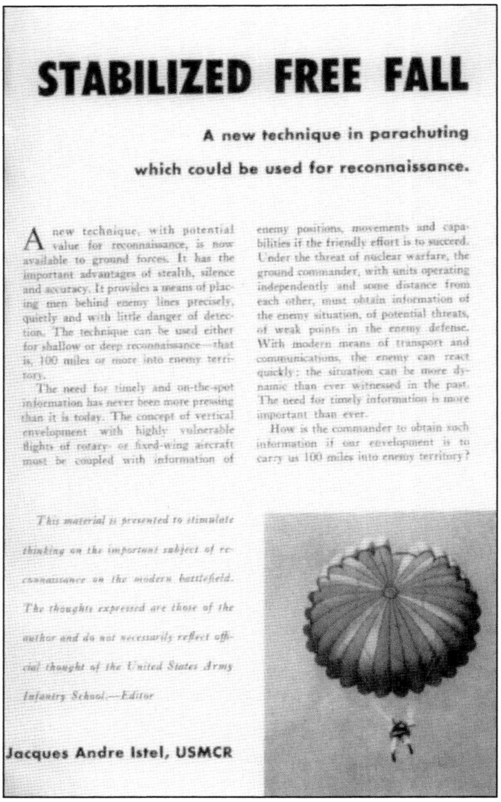

STABILIZED FREE FALL

A new technique in parachuting which could be used for reconnaissance.

A new technique, with potential value for reconnaissance, is now available to ground forces. It has the important advantages of stealth, silence and accuracy. It provides a means of placing men behind enemy lines precisely, quietly and with little danger of detection. The technique can be used either for shallow or deep reconnaissance—that is, 100 miles or more into enemy territory.

The need for timely and on-the-spot information has never been more pressing than it is today. The concept of vertical envelopment with highly vulnerable flights of rotary- or fixed-wing aircraft must be coupled with information of enemy positions, movements and capabilities if the friendly effort is to succeed. Under the threat of nuclear warfare, the ground commander, with units operating independently and some distance from each other, must obtain information of the enemy situation, of potential threats, of weak points in the enemy defense. With modern means of transport and communications, the enemy can react quickly; the situation can be more dynamic than ever witnessed in the past. The need for timely information is more important than ever.

How is the commander to obtain such information if our envelopment is to carry us 100 miles into enemy territory?

This material is presented to stimulate thinking on the important subject of reconnaissance on the modern battlefield. The thoughts expressed are those of the author and do not necessarily reflect official thought of the United States Army Infantry School.—Editor

Jacques Andre Istel, USMCR

MILITARY FREE FALL BEGINNINGS. After World War II, Lt. Col. Jacques Andre Istel, a captain at the time with the US Marine Corps Reserves, started the first commercial free fall school, Parachutes Inc. Istel conducted demonstrations to convince the military to utilize free fall for stealth insertion. In 1957, members of the Army's special forces attended a military free fall course instructed by Parachutes Inc. at Fort Bragg. In 1958, Lieutenant Colonel Istel began instructing military free fall methods to the first Marine Corps Force Recon Company. Military free fall was now part of military operations. The page from the *Infantry* magazine of January 1958 at left captures a HALO jump at Fort Bragg in November 1957 by Istel. Below, the history of Parachutes Inc. is recorded at the Museum of History in Granite in Felicity, California. (Left, courtesy of the US Army; below, courtesy of the Museum of History in Granite.)

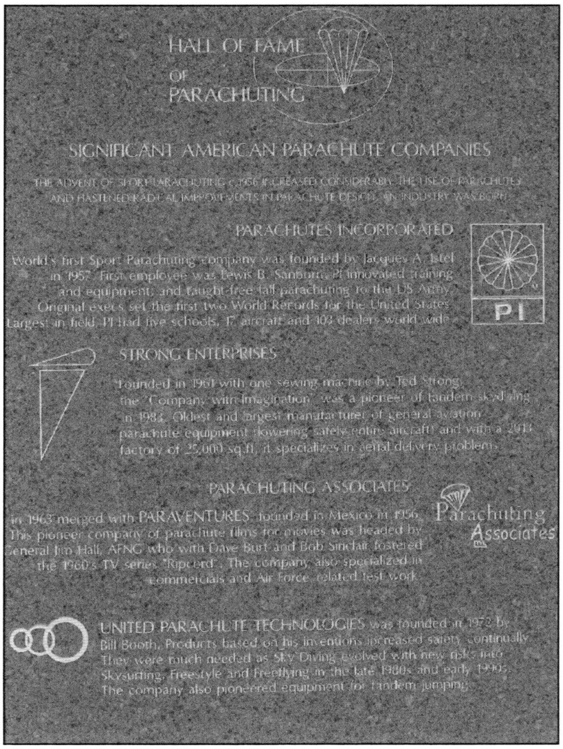

THE MILITARY FREE FALL SCHOOL . In 1958, Lieutenant Colonel Istel's vision of military free fall had come to life. After his training with members of the Army's special forces at Fort Bragg on high-altitude, low opening (HALO), he further demonstrated and conducted stabilization free fall training. In 1958, the Army conducted its first HALO test class at the Yuma Test Station. In this photograph, from left to right, are (first row) Sergeant 1st Class Goodrid, Sergeant 1st Class Hiese, and Master Sergeant Glenn; (second row) Captain Peterka, Chief Warrant Officer Turner, Sergeant 1st Class Williamson, Specialist Broussad, and Specialist Pennington. (Courtesy of the US Army.)

THE GOLDEN KNIGHTS. In 1959, the Army named Gen. Joseph Stilwell Jr. to form the Strategic Army Command Parachute Team to compete in the new sport of skydiving. The founding members of the team were students of Lieutenant Colonel Istel. In 1961, the Department of Defense established the US Army Parachute Team. In 1962, the team was nicknamed "Golden Knights" to represent the gold medals they won in the new sport. The Golden Knights are one of three Department of Defense aerial demonstration teams. On March 25, 1997, Pres. George Bush Sr. conducted a free fall jump with the Golden Knights following training at the Military Free Fall School, Yuma Proving Ground. Above, General Stilwell talks with Maj. Gen. Curtis E. LeMay of the 20th Bomber Command in 1945. At left is an Army Golden Knight during Armed Forces Day in 1941 at Grand Folks Air Force Base. (Both, courtesy of the National Archives.)

Eight

Yuma Proving Ground

The transition of the Yuma Test Station in 1951 to the Yuma Proving Ground in 1963 was more than expanding its mission of ranges and testing. A part of the US Army's reorganization and structuring, the facility was placed under the control of the US Army Material Command—the Army's Test and Evaluation Command. This new reorganization increased the station's mission for testing equipment for the Army.

Since 1963, the Yuma Proving Ground has not only supported the local economy of Yuma, but has also continued to be the premier facility for testing equipment for the Department of Defense and other government organizations, with open airspace, large ranges, and a supporting climate.

Over the years, Yuma Proving Ground has seen NATO weapon system testing, NASA testing, the development of an armament range (Cibola Range), the development of GPS, testing of the M1 Abrams tank, and testing of the Bradley Fighting Vehicle, as well as numerous other systems. The Yuma Proving Ground has been instrumental in support of the nation's military.

Since its origins in World War II, the Yuma Proving Ground continues to provide one of four global locations for military testing and troop training in the desert environment. The Yuma Proving Ground has conducted environment testing since its expansions in 1948. To test equipment in various natural environments, the Yuma Proving Ground conducts military testing at three locations: Yuma Test Center (Arizona), Cold Regions Test Center (Alaska), and the Tropic Regions Test Center (Panama, Honduras, Suriname, and Hawaii).

Yuma Proving Ground Entry Sign. Located where Camp Laguna once stood, the Yuma Proving Ground sign not only signals the public traveling through the area to be cautious, it also celebrates the proving ground's history. (Author's collection.)

Lunar Rover Mobility Test. In 1966, NASA conducted mobility tests at the Yuma Proving Ground for the wheels for the lunar rover vehicle. The lunar rover was developed to allow astronauts to travel greater distances on the lunar surface. Testing of mesh wheels led to development changes. Several prototypes were tested at the Yuma Proving Ground, with two shown here: wire mesh by GM (above) and hoop spring by Bendix (below). (Both, courtesy of the US Army.)

Artillery and Tank Munitions. In the Army, artillery is known as the "king of battle" because of its ability to produce a large number of casualties. The Yuma Proving Ground has been the Army's primary testing site for artillery systems over the years. One type of artillery weapon system is the howitzer, a weapon that propels projectiles at high trajectories. Howitzers can be either towed or self-propelled. In the photograph above, a self-propelled 105mm Howitzer negotiates an opening on a bridge during summer environmental testing. Below, an Ultra Lightweight Howitzer is tested at the Yuma Proving Ground. (Both, courtesy of the US Army.)

Ranges and Weapon Testing. As the Yuma Proving Ground expanded to conduct tests of explosive ordnance, weapons and equipment testing was conducted on the King of Arizona (KOFA) range area. In the photograph above, a Short Stop Howitzer is test fired on September 26, 1992. The photograph below is of a LAV (light armored vehicle) air defense system being tested in the 1980s. (Both, courtesy of the US Army.)

VEHICLE TESTING. With over 200 miles of road courses for wheeled and tracked vehicles, the Yuma Proving Ground is a military automotive test facility for the desert environment. In the photograph above is the M88A1 recovery vehicle being tested as it tows an Abrams tank on October 30, 1987. The M88 recovery vehicle is used to extricate damaged vehicles that cannot be repaired on-site. First developed in 1961 from components of the M48 and M60 tanks, it continued in operations with the M88A1 in 1977 and the M88A2 in 1997. Below, an Abrams tank conducts a mobility road test. (Both, courtesy of the US Army.)

Dust Course. Part of the Yuma Proving Ground's mobility testing site is the dust course that tests the effects of the environment on equipment. Above, an Abrams tank travels through the dust course in 1986. Below, a prototype XMP Abrams conducts a test as part of the research and development section in 1976. (Both, courtesy of the US Army.)

AMMUNITION TESTING. After World War II, the Army began conducting research on shaped charges to defeat enemy armor. The Shillelagh was one of the missiles tested at the Yuma Proving Ground that led to the development of guided missiles. In the photograph above, an M551 Sheridan Armored Reconnaissance/Airborne Assault Vehicle fires the Shillelagh. Below, the M551 fires a conventional round. The M551 was a light tank, capable of being delivered by air and traversing rivers. It was named after Civil War general Philip Sheridan. (Both, courtesy of the US Army.)

ARMORED TANK TESTING. The M1 tank began production at Chrysler in 1979. In 1985, the M1A1 began production and continued until 1992. The M1A1 Abrams tank consisted of 14 wheels, shock absorbers, and additional armor. During testing, the Abrams negotiated the 60-degree slope, crossed water obstacles at 1.21 meters, climbed obstacles of 1.06 meters, and crossed trenches of 2.74 meters. In the above photograph, an Abrams throws a track during testing in 1986. Below, an Abrams traverses a water obstacle. (Both, courtesy of the US Army.)

MUNITIONS AND WEAPONS TESTING. Helicopter armament, munitions, and target acquisition systems are all tested at the Yuma Proving Ground. The photograph above shows testing of missile capabilities in 1987. Below is the 16-inch naval gun program subtest in 1986. (Both, courtesy of the US Army.)

Aerial Projectile Burst Testing. The aerial burst program was to test dispersion and penetration of projectiles. The tests were conducted at set heights to simulate aerial drops. The photograph above is of an airburst test. The image below is of the direct hit by a target-seeking unguided 155mm projectile as part of the Selected Target Activated Fire and Forget (STAFF) program. (Both, courtesy of the US Army.)

AIRBORNE TESTING ACTIVITY. In 1958, the Army transferred its air delivery mission to the airborne test activity (airdrop qualification of ammunition and development of personnel) at the Yuma Proving Ground. The large areas for drop zones and existing testing capabilities including the Laguna Army Airfield complex made Yuma the right choice. Directly following the transfer of the airborne test activity, the first Army free fall school was established at Yuma Proving Ground. At left is the testing of air transport on July 8, 1997. Below is an XM1 tank being loaded onto a C-5A aircraft in 1980. (Both, courtesy of the US Army.)

Airborne Airdrop Testing. Located on the north side of the training areas, the Yuma Proving Ground tested the ACES 2 Aircraft Controlled Exit System on July 17, 1982, conducting a 30,000-foot airdrop with four connected platforms, two 28-foot extraction chutes, and a 100-foot G-11A main chute. The c. 1980 picture below shows airdrops taking place at the Yuma Proving Ground. (Both, courtesy of the US Army.)

Airdrop Parachute and Control Testing. Conducting tests for parachutes and guided systems, the Yuma Proving Ground is a test facility for air delivery systems. With good flying conditions, the Yuma Proving Ground has 12 drop zones. At left, a low-altitude retrorocket system (LARRS) is tested on May 11, 1993. Below is a High Mobility Multipurpose Wheeled Vehicle (HMMWV) airdrop test conducted on May 10, 1988. (Both, courtesy of the US Army.)

Air Delivery Systems. The Low-Altitude Parachute Extraction System (LAPES) was developed for combat operations, allowing the delivery of supplies to units in the field. As a group parachutes into enemy territory, their vehicles are delivered by LAPES. Above, in 1969, a C130 conducts a LAPES test at the Yuma Proving Ground. Below, a C130 delivers an HMMWV during a LAPES test on April 7, 1988. (Both, courtesy of the US Army.)

Military Free Fall Parachute Testing. With the vision of Lt. Col. Jacques Andre Istil of military free fall a reality, a demonstration for Pres. John F. Kennedy was conducted by the Army in 1961. In 1962, the first official HALO course was conducted. Throughout the 1960s, tests for various systems for airborne operations were also conducted. In 1995, the Military Free Fall School was permanently assigned to the Yuma Proving Ground. The school operates under the control of the US Army Special Operations Command's John F. Kennedy Special Warfare Center and School. The Military Free Fall School conducts multiple training courses, including Military Free Fall Parachutist, Military Free Fall Jumpmaster, and Military Free Fall Advanced Tactical Infiltration. Being an advanced training facility, the school utilizes a wind tunnel for ground training. This photograph shows testing of a box kite on September 23, 1994. (Courtesy of Yuma Proving Ground Heritage Center.)

Photographic Testing Equipment. The Yuma Proving Ground utilizes special photographic equipment to gather data during testing. This data provides critical information that might not have been otherwise captured. The photographic equipment has also incidentally captured the history of the Yuma Proving Ground, without which this book would not have existed. The photograph above is of a photo optics camera. Below is a camera system that overlooks the Yuma Proving Ground. (Both, courtesy of the US Army.)

The Global Positioning System. The Precision Automated Tracking System (PATS) was part of the US Air Force Navigation System using Timing and Ranging (NAVSTAR) brought to the Yuma Proving Ground in 1973 to test advanced ordnance systems. Above, Sen. Barry Goldwater is seen with military personnel testing the system. PATS measured elevation, range, and azimuth. The system sent signals to retroreflectors from the ground, as seen on the aircraft at left. It was the initial navigation test program to support NAVSTAR. In 1974, the Defense Mapping Agency conducted a geodetic survey in support of Global Positioning System (GPS) tests at the Yuma Proving Ground. In 1978, the ground systems were replaced with a satellite network. Today, GPS is well known as a navigation system for the commercial and public sectors. (Both, courtesy of the US Army.)

Nine

Into the Future

Today, the Yuma Proving Ground is one of the largest military installations, with more than 1,430 square miles that serve approximately 17,000 personnel a year with a mission to "plan, conduct, analyze, report and support development tests, production phases and integrated developmental/operational tests; and provide training support to Army, sister services, Department of Defense, US Government, international, and commercial customers."

The majority of the units on Yuma Proving Ground are attached to major commands. For example, the personnel at the health clinic are assigned to the Weed Army Community Hospital at Fort Irwin and the Light Armored Vehicle Test Directorate is a Marine Corps detachment.

Of all the operations at Yuma Proving Ground, perhaps it is best known for the Amy's elite Military Free Fall School where the public often watches as elite special operations personnel jump in HALO and HAHO operations along Martinez Lake Road, which leads from US Route 95 to Fishers Landing, a small resort on the Colorado River.

The Yuma Proving Ground is a research and development installation that utilizes the scientific method to gather data and determine results. Employees assigned to the Yuma Proving Ground come from various backgrounds, including the science and engineering fields. Based upon observations, testing at Yuma Proving Ground has had significant positive effects on industry.

From the early days of the frontier, the US Army has had a presence in the desert regions of Yuma. From setting the boundaries of the United States with Mexico to western expansion across the Colorado River, the Army continues to lead change into the future. The Yuma Proving Ground continues its proud history as a part of the Army.

Mine Systems. The Yuma Proving Ground conducts tests on land mines and mine removal systems. The center also has specialized facilities for testing countermeasures to Improvised Explosive Devices (IED), conducting research to save the lives of soldiers. This photograph shows an HMMWV that was hit by an IED from a roadside explosion while the 160th Infantry was conducting combat operations in Iraq in 2008. Research from countermeasure testing of IEDs created data that provided information for armor placement, preventing penetration of IEDs into the compartment area of the vehicle. (Author's collection.)

A Host to Other Agencies. The Yuma Proving Ground also hosts other government agencies and contractors. The two most widely known are the Department of Homeland Security and General Motors. The white aerostat balloon seen hovering above the mountains on the Yuma Proving Ground is operated by the Department of Homeland Security. The balloon conducts surveillance of the airspace along the international border. In 2009, General Motors moved its desert automotive testing facility from Mesa, Arizona, to the Yuma Proving Ground, which had been operating since 1953. The new facility has a track that automotive testers can utilize year-round. (Both, author's collection.)

ADVANCED DRONES. The most publicized drone test recently at the Yuma Proving Ground was the subsonic XQ-58A Valkyrie in 2019. At left is an unmanned aerial vehicle (UAV) being tested on June 30, 1992, at Yuma. Below is the XQ-58A Valkyrie, designed by Kratos Defense & Security Systems (Left, courtesy of the US Army; below, courtesy of the US Air Force.)

THE YUMA PROVING GROUND HERITAGE MUSEUM. The Yuma Proving Ground Heritage Museum is located on the military installation. Request for public access to the museum is processed through security at the outdoor exhibit. Pictured above is the outdoor Wahner E. Brooks historical exhibit, open to the public off East Imperial Dam Road west of Highway 95 across from the Yuma Proving Ground. (Both, courtesy of the US Army.)

Bibliography

Ainsworth, Katherine. *The Man Who Captured Sunshine*. Palm Springs, CA: Etc Publications, 1978.

Davidson, Bill. "Desert Warfare: America Trains a New Kind of Army." *Yank*. September 23, 1942.

Bischoff, Matt C. *The Desert Training Center/ California–Arizona Maneuver Area, 1942–1944: Historical and Archaeological Contexts*. Redlands, CA: Statistical Research Inc., 2006.

Burney, James. *A Chronological History of the Discoveries in the South Sea or Pacific Ocean*. New York, NY: Cambridge University Press, 2010.

Decker, Oscar C. "The Patton Tanks: The Cold War Learning Series." *Camp Colt to Desert Storm: The History of US Armored Forces*. Lexington, KY: University Press of Kentucky, 1999.

Fredricksen, John C. *Fighting Elites: A History of U.S. Special Forces*. Santa Barbara, CA: ABC-CLIO, 2011.

Heidner, Bill. *Camp Laguna*. Yuma, AZ: Yuma Proving Ground Heritage Center, 2009.

———. *Preparing for War in the Desert Southwest*. Yuma, AZ: Yuma Proving Ground Heritage Center, 2011.

Henley, David C. *The Land That God Forgot: The Saga of Gen. George Patton's Desert Training Camp*. Fallon, NV: Western Military History Association, 1992.

Hunter, Louis C. *Steamboats on the Western Rivers*. New York, NY: Dover Publications, 1947.

Istel, Jacques Andre. "Airborne Operations." *Infantry*. United States Army Infantry School. January, 1958.

Laverty, Scott L. *United States of America Army National Guard Officer Candidate School*. Dana Point, CA: CreateSpace, 2016.

Lingenfelter, Richard E. *Steamboats on the Colorado River, 1852–1916*. Tucson, AZ: University of Arizona Press, 1978.

Meller, Sidney. *The Desert Training Center and C-AMA–Study #15*. Washington, DC: Historical Section, Army Ground Forces, 1946.

Meyers, Bruce F. *Fortune Favors the Brave: The Story of First Force Recon*. Annapolis, MD: Naval Institute Press, 2000.

Shamburger, John. "Project OTTER: Overland Train Terrain Evaluation Research." *Technical Review* No. 3-588, US Army Corps of Engineers. December 1961.

Stanton, Shelby L. *US Army Uniforms of World War II*. Mechanicsburg, PA: Stackpole Books, 1995.

US Army Yuma Proving Ground. *Final Range Wide Environmental Impact Statement*. Phoenix, AZ: Command Technology Directorate, 2001.

US Department of the Interior. *Desert Training Center*. Bureau of Land Management, 1985.

About the Organization

From its early stages, the Yuma Proving Ground Heritage Center has captured the history of the people and events that made the installation what it is today—a premier US Army testing and training facility. The center interprets military culture through galleries that record the history of the Yuma Training Ground. It presents a visual interpretation of the history of the Desert Training Center, Camp Laguna, Camp Seeley, the Yuma Test Branch, the Yuma Test Station, and the Yuma Proving Ground.

The Heritage Center not only preserves the history, it supports the memory of all those who have transitioned through the installation to protect this great country. As the Heritage Center states, "remember that the real story is about people . . . people who trained here and people who worked to research, develop, test, and evaluate the tools our nation's military personnel used to protect our country and freedoms."

Today, the Yuma Proving Ground Heritage Center captures its history through a visual representation at the museum. It is the only Army installation that holds and displays a significant portion of its history. The museum hosts more than 6,000 people each year from around the world. Currently, M.Sgt. William Heidner (Ret.) is the museum curator.

For more information or to visit the Heritage Center, visit the Visitor Control Center on Imperial Dam Road across from the Yuma Proving Ground main facility.